CONTENTS

KT-527-059

FOREWORD

by Cameron Mackintosh

The greatest praise for a good stage manager is that the audience never knows they exist! Yet from the moment the House lights go down, the person running 'the corner', which is literally the heart (and brain!) of a show whilst it is playing, controls and commands every department which, on a good night, seamlessly works together to make what happens on stage both effortless and magical! Everyone backstage has a vital job to do and a good stage manager is the linchpin, and it requires someone with a quick mind and brilliant timing as well as a firm but kindly disposition that combines discipline with fun so that everyone has a good time as they give a good show.

This is particularly important with a musical where both the numbers of people and the technical requirements of moving large amounts of scenery, often at lightning speed, need split-second timing and a really artistic touch. The cues of the various departments under the control of the stage manager are all marked in a script known as 'the book' but with a busy show, a really good stage manager will sense the tempo of the performance and subtly anticipate or delay these marked cues like a concert pianist bringing to life a concerto.

However, the person running the corner, though he or she has their finger on the button, is only one vitally important member of the team and it is the way that the team works together that keeps the show running smoothly.

They have to depend on each other instinctively and when things go wrong, as live theatre often does, they need to all think on their feet, both to avoid accidents and also keep the performance going if at all possible. This takes a huge amount of hard work and the mark of a good stage management team is that it is not just work but a vocation. They are invariably the first people to get into the theatre in the morning and the last to leave at night. The running of the shows change like shifting sands and the good stage managers never get bored because of it. No two days are ever the same: no two shows are ever the same. Cast and crew invariably change their personnel and part of the stage manager's job is to ensure that this in no way affects what the audience is seeing.

In itself, stage managing can be a very fulfilling career but often, as it was in my case, it is the perfect training ground for moving into other areas of the theatre or entertainment business. I know that as a producer myself, having done virtually every job backstage, it has helped me immeasurably in understanding how to put together a show and the importance of theatrical design in literally 'choreographing' the visual interest and dramatic build of an evening. When I started, I got paid an all inclusive £17 per week to work as many hours as the producer required – no overtime! Things are a bit better now, but I have always been grateful for the huge variety of jobs I experienced through the slavery! In today's world, a stage manager has to be aware of so many different aspects of a show. Technical advancements backstage have made incredible leaps in the past 10–15 years but you need to control it, not become its victim. When I started 35 years ago, the words Health and Safety meant 'get out of the way' if a sandbag plummeted from the Flies, but just as important as grasping the new techniques is an ability to communicate with charm, humour and firmness with every department backstage, so that everyone from the temporary dresser to the Master Carpenter feels that without them the show won't go on properly.

Soozie and Philippa's book gives tremendous insight into every aspect of a stage manager's job and they have communicated their depth of knowledge in a wonderful accessible way which I am sure will be invaluable to anyone considering this as a career.

Good luck and many happy openings.

INTRODUCTION

WHAT IS STAGE MANAGEMENT ABOUT?

A frequently asked question to us both ... 'but what does a stage manager actually do? If they are not responsible for the lighting, sound, direction, costumes, acting, make-up, box office or choreography, what could there possibly be left for them to do?' The answer to this question is, in fact, 'a great deal'. A stage manager's job is complex to describe and almost impossible to define. By guiding you through a journey of exploration this book will give you an insight into the world of the stage manager and their team. By following the process of putting on a show from the stage manager's point of view, we will illustrate how a stage manager is involved in almost every aspect of a production. A show can mean anything from a single performer in a back room of a pub to a cast of 500 performing the passion play at Oberammergau. It can be a modern comedy by Alan Ayckbourn or a tragedy by William Shakespeare, a new ballet by London Contemporary Dance Company, a children's show by David Wood, a cabaret or an old-time music hall. It may be performed in a church hall, an ancient outdoor amphitheatre or the stage of a world famous theatre, but whatever the content and wherever the venue you can be sure someone will be stage managing! It is this varied and exciting role that we hope to reveal to you through the chapters of this book and by answering the question 'What do you actually do?' We hope to infect you with our enthusiasm for a fascinating and demanding job.

Stage management covers every aspect of a production, from the acting company to the props and furniture. **Guildhall School of Music and Drama, The Workshop.** *Photo: Laurence Burns*

1 THE WORKPLACE

All aspects of theatre present challenges to a stage manager. If you are able to work in many different types of theatre, especially early on in your career you will gain valuable experience across a broad range of the industry as well as having the opportunity to discover which type of theatre most interests you. The theatre world is very varied and within the industry there are a number of different companies providing the stage manager with a multitude of working experiences.

Whichever form of theatre grabs your interest, the basic job of stage managing remains the same and the skills and knowledge illustrated in this book will be applicable to a large opera company touring the world as well as a small experimental fringe production performed in the back room of a pub. Newspapers and trade magazines are useful to read and will give you a good understanding of the broad range of modern theatre. One of the most widely read trade newspapers in the United Kingdom is *The Stage*, and *Plays International* will give you an idea of worldwide productions. If you have access to the Internet a good site is www.theatredesign.org.uk, which has many links to other theatre-related websites.

REPERTORY THEATRE

Repertory or regional theatres are usually known as rep theatre. Rep theatres present plays on a one-off basis. Sometimes these plays are produced by the theatre's management, sometimes they are a co-production with another theatre and sometimes they are imported or toured in from another company. Wherever the production has originated from it will be available for a limited period only. This may be two, three or even six weeks but is more usually three to four weeks. After the specified time the production will no longer be performed. The set and costumes are usually destroyed or returned to the hire companies and all the elements of the production are disbanded. The next production's first night is usually within a week of the last night and the whole cycle starts again. There is an almost continuous flow of productions one after another at approximately three to four-weekly intervals. This means that at any one time there are three to four productions at various stages – one show in production, one show in rehearsal and one show nearing the end of the planning stage. The fourth production may well be being cast or initial designs and so on being discussed.

A typical season runs from mid-August, through Christmas, into the late spring of the following year. Therefore your contract can be for a full nine months and is often renewed in early summer for the start of the next season. Working in a repertory theatre can provide great variety in terms of the type of plays you work on and a feeling of continuity as you remain in one place and are working for the same people for a reasonable length of time. The acting company is unlikely to stay the same as most actors will only be employed for one or two plays within the season, but the resident staff such as painters, electricians, wardrobe and administration staff will be more permanent.

A Selection of Well-Established Regional Theatre Companies in the UK

Birmingham Repertory Company
Salisbury Playhouse
Chichester Festival Theatre
West Yorkshire Playhouse
Theatre Clwyd
Royal Exchange Manchester
Bristol Old Vic
Leicester Haymarket

COMMERCIAL AND SUBSIDIZED THEATRE

Commercial theatre receives no subsidy from the Arts Council and relies purely on profits from selling tickets and money from sponsorship and investors, to remain in business. This influences the type of production offered by a commercial theatre and therefore the nature of the stage manager's job. The type of play or musical chosen will be made in order to attract the largest audience and the casting will also be influenced by the need for the production to make a profit. This means that stage management will be working under tight financial criteria and with actors who have different temperaments to actors who may have only just entered the profession. Commercial theatre spends a lot of money on large and spectacular productions with large and starry casts. The production is either based exclusively in the West End or is taken out on a long tour to large theatres. This necessarily produces a different working atmosphere that can be very exciting,

Salisbury Playhouse, currently a leading regional repertory theatre.

(Above) The spacious and modern box office at Salisbury Playhouse. The two clocks on the back wall are used to indicate the finishing times for the performances in the main house and the studio theatre.

London Apollo Hammersmith: a famous London commercial theatre.

Some Well-Known UK Commercial Managements

E&B Productions (Theatre) Ltd
Apollo Leisure (UK) Ltd
Bill Kenwright Ltd
Cameron Mackintosh Ltd

The Really Useful Group Ltd
The Robert Stigwood Organization Ltd
Kenneth H. Wax Ltd
Duncan C. Weldon Productions Ltd

exhausting and demanding. Theatre in the 'West End' of London is almost exclusively commercial theatre.

Subsidized theatre means that the company receives a grant from the Arts Council to cover some of the costs. They are therefore not so reliant on selling tickets and can produce plays that may not have so great a popular appeal. They do not necessarily have to employ a famous actor to attract an audience or they may be able to present the play in an unusual or controversial style.

TOURING THEATRE

Stage management in touring theatre tends to be contracted to work on one play at a time. The rehearsal period is slightly longer and the play will tour from six weeks to six months and sometimes longer. Some commercial tours last over a year. Sometimes the play visits a new town every week, sometimes every two weeks. There is also the opportunity to travel abroad to almost any country in the world – particularly countries where the British Council operates.

A touring company is a self-contained unit and the stage management have more responsibilities for the company than they would in a repertory theatre. The company are together for a much longer time forming a close-knit group and tend to stick together in a strange town or country. The company rely on each other much more than they would if they were going home each night after the show. The company stage manager in particular becomes something of a mother or father figure and must have well-developed people skills as well as the technical skills required to reproduce the show for each venue. There is also small-scale touring involving performing for a few nights at each venue. This is usually in small school halls, studio theatres or community centres rather than the large touring theatres that the subsidized and commercial tours visit.

> **A Typical List of Touring Dates on a Middle Scale UK Tour**
>
> Buxton Opera House
> Brewhouse Theatre, Taunton
> Theatre Royal, Bath
> Oxford Playhouse Theatre
> Harlow Playhouse
> Towngate Theatre, Poole
> The Hexagon, Reading
> Sunderland Empire
> The Mayflower Theatre, Southampton
> New Theatre, Hull
> Kings Theatre, Edinburgh

FRINGE THEATRE

Fringe theatre traditionally provides small-scale productions, often run on a co-operative basis where all those working on the production take a share of the profits if there are any. The work performed is often new writing or established texts presented in a new or controversial way. There is rarely a full stage management team and very often the stage manager doubles as an electrician as well. It can be a very challenging environment in which to work and very exciting especially when working on a new play which has never been performed before. However, you do need to be a master of all trades and be truly dedicated to your art, sometimes working long hours for very little money. Technical equipment is usually quite basic and a hands-on approach is necessary. Stage managing in the fringe theatre is quite different from other theatre forms but many stage managers enjoy getting fully involved and rising to the challenge.

CHILDREN'S THEATRE

Children's theatre involves performing plays often written specifically for children. There

Some Well-Known and Respected London Fringe Theatres

Almeida
BAC (Battersea Arts Centre)
Bridewell
Donmar Warehouse
Hampstead
Kings Head
Old Red Lion
Riverside Studios
Tricycle Theatre

are a few specialist children's theatre companies or you may be involved in theatre for children through the education department of the theatre you work for. One of the main differences is that the performance times are usually through the day, particularly on Saturday mornings or during school hours. A children's audience is very different from an adult audience and often the work involves taking the play to the audience rather than the children coming to your base theatre.

Working with children, who are part of the cast performing alongside adults, provides stage management with different challenges. The stage manager needs to be familiar with the law restricting the hours that children are allowed to work. In the UK this information can usually be obtained from the local education authority. They need to understand the conditions under which children are allowed to work, such as how many hours at a time and any safety regulations applicable to employing children. This usually means two teams of children to cover all the necessary performances and a team of chaperones to look after them.

Working with children and working in children's theatre are two very different things. Many stage managers will work with children at some point in their careers, others will choose to work in children's theatre because they are attracted to that particular type of theatre.

OPERA

The ability to read music is essential if you wish to work in the world of opera. Compared to a straight play, an opera is a spectacular and lavish production. The company will be much larger than most acting companies and there is a clear division between the principals and the chorus members. It is not unusual for an opera company to number one hundred people or more excluding the orchestra. There are more people involved backstage because productions tend to be more complex with large and heavy sets or many scenes requiring lots of scene changes. Generally a stage crew will be employed and the stage manager will have to deal with répétiteurs, conductors, assistant directors, orchestral managers, choreographers and costume designers, in addition to the usual creative team of director, designer and lighting designer involved in mounting a stage play.

A common aspect of an opera production is the numerous nationalities that take part. The opera world is very much an international one, with many different nationalities involved both onstage and backstage. The ability to speak a foreign language could be very useful to a stage manager although this is by no means essential. One advantage of working in opera is that there are no consecutive performances. The demands on an opera singer's voice in singing for one performance make it impossible for them to sing on two consecutive nights and definitely no matinées. If you were involved backstage with two different operas for the same company or performing at the same venue it is possible that you may work consecutive nights but this is unlikely and most opera stage managers work one night on and one night off!

Guildhall School of Music and Drama's production of **Pippi Longstocking,** *a typical fantastical fast-moving show, particularly suitable for children.* Photo: Laurence Burns

(Above) The chorus of The Tsarina's Shoes, *Guildhall School of Music and Drama.*

The chorus of The Tsarina's Shoes *in a crowd scene. Note that each member had an extensive costume including shawls and hats. Guildhall School of Music and Drama.*

MUSICALS

In common with opera, musicals tend to be lavish, spectacular productions, often with a large cast or a chorus of dancers. The style, story and music obviously vary as much as any stage play, but the sets and costumes are usually more complicated and expensive than would be required for a play. Whilst opera relies on the music and the unique voices of the singers to

provide the spectacle a musical often employs fantastic special effects and magical scene changes. A stage manager on a musical must have sound technical knowledge as well as good people skills. They will need to be comfortable dealing with large casts, some of which will include very famous names, and all the press and publicity issues that come with such a cast. An ability to read music is a distinct advantage although one stage manager successfully cued a famous production of My Fair Lady without being able to read a note of music. She instinctively 'felt' the right points to give the cues because she had an understanding of the music without actually reading it note by note. The cost of producing a musical is very high, which inevitably means that commercial managements produce them. Two of the most successful impresarios in the musical world today are Cameron Mackintosh and Andrew Lloyd Webber, who between them have produced nearly all of the successful musicals for the last thirty years. In order to recover the production costs musicals usually have very long runs. This may

(Above) **The Tsarina's Shoes** *chorus on-stage with specific icon props that needed to be set accurately in the wings to ensure that the right chorus member carried the right icon.* Guildhall School of Music and Drama.

OPPOSITE PAGE
(Top) Guildhall School of Music and Drama's production of **Grand Hotel***. Note the shiny floor which stage management had to keep polished without it being slippery.*

(Bottom) Dance number from the musical **Little Me***, Guildhall School of Music and Drama. Director Martin Connor, Designer Mark Bailey, Choreographer Bill Deamer, Lighting Designer David Kidd.*

include a long tour prior to a West End run, which in some cases has been as long as ten years or more. Some musicals have closed shortly after coming into the West End because the audiences have been very small.

2 THE TEAM

The stage management team forms a vital nerve centre, bringing together all the production technical departments, commonly known as the staging departments. Stage management needs to be fluid, dealing with every task, situation and person that may come their way.

An elderly actor, who has since departed from this world, once said to an eager young student desperate to be a good head of their team, 'before you become a good stage manager, you will need to take on the role of mother, father, teacher, comic, nursemaid, judge and confessor all rolled into one'. The elderly actor was so right, but his piece of valuable advice also applies to the rest of the team; stage management has to handle the company, creative team, technicians and heads of department in all moods and situations. They have to do this with sensitivity, understanding, tact and diplomacy, and above all need to have a great sense of humour. Putting all the above into a melting pot with a love of people and a passion for the job, will produce a good solid stage management team.

TEAM TITLES

The stage management team consists of three people – the Stage Manager, the Deputy Stage Manager and the Assistant Stage Manager. These names are always abbreviated to SM/DSM/ASM.

If a production is large and complex, there may be an addition to the team of an extra ASM or two, and in some cases a second DSM, but there is always only one SM. Regardless of the size of production, the job aspects of each team member are virtually the same.

WHAT EACH MEMBER OF THE TEAM DOES AND WHY

The Stage Manager

SM Qualities
- Passion for the job
- Love and understanding of people
- Caring
- Patience and tolerance
- Ability to work as part of a team
- Ability to work solo
- Ability to take responsibility
- Not afraid of hard work and long hours
- Sense of humour
- Ability to laugh at yourself
- Energy
- Tenacity
- Awareness of others
- Sensitivity and understanding of others
- Ability to be a good listener
- Ability to be a good communicator
- Ability to give and take instruction
- Ability to be a good organizer
- Ability to be a good note-taker
- Being methodical and systematic
- An awareness of technical theatre
- Practical ability

The stage manager has an interesting and fulfilling job. They work closely with the director, company, set and costume designer, lighting designer and sound designer who are all known as the creative team; if applicable, there may also be choreographers, voice and movement coaches. The stage manager also works closely with the theatre's own teams known as the staging departments. These are lighting electricians, sound technicians, carpenters, painters and wardrobe staff. The stage manager is a very important person within the theatre structure. Their role is extremely varied, making it a multi-tasking and multi-thinking job. The SM is responsible for 'managing', as the title implies, the show and the stage.

They attend all rehearsals and meetings, and are a liaison officer between the staging departments. They work closely with the DSM, submitting to them any necessary information from the staging departments and creative teams, and in return receiving and passing on any rehearsal notes. Ensuring nothing escapes their attention, the stage manager must maintain this communication on a regular day-to-day basis. The SM attends rehearsals at least three times a day and arranges a meeting with the whole team at the end of rehearsal to exchange information.

They delegate the necessary jobs to the ASM whether it's sweeping the rehearsal room floor, finding, borrowing or making props, making sure the ASM is clear in what is happening and that they have understood all instructions, thereby eliminating any potential frustration, angst and time-wasting hours.

The SM needs to be sure that necessary resources are available, find rehearsal space, props and furniture, and attend to the needs and requirements of director, company, fight director, choreographer and musical director throughout the rehearsal process. You need to keep a sharp eye on the progress of the production, and gain knowledge of the artistic intentions of the director and designer, never allowing anything to grow out of proportion with the original design concept and budget agreement.

SM Job

- Running the team
- Delegating
- Working closely with the DSM and ASM
- Dealing with the company and their needs
- Working closely with the creative team
- Liaison Officer to all staging departments
- Finding and booking rehearsal rooms
- Marking out the set design on the rehearsal room floor
- Setting up the rehearsal room each day
- Daily visits to the rehearsal room while the rehearsal is in progress
- Making lists of prop and furniture positions, scene changes, etc.
- Keeping a regular update on all changes coming out of rehearsals and all paperwork
- Reaching deadlines with all paperwork
- Using computers, phones and faxes
- Organizing costume fittings, rehearsal calls, fight or dance calls
- Attending all production meetings
- Overseeing and sometimes being part of finding props/furniture/set dressings
- Keeping a check on the budget of both your own and other departments
- Keeping a stage management petty cash float and accounting for how it is spent
- Keeping a check and liaising with the Marketing/Publicity department on all necessary publicity calls, cast list details/trade credits/staff lists/collection of cast biographies and photos, etc.
- Running all final run-throughs in a rehearsal room
- Organizing the transfer from the rehearsal room to the stage
- Setting up the stage for Technical rehearsals and running them
- Running all Dress rehearsals into the previews and press nights
- Running the first performance to the last
- Putting the show away at the end of its run

The Three Sisters, *Guildhall School of Music and Drama. This piece is challenging for stage management because it requires period Russian props including toys.* Photo: *Laurence Burns*

The Workroom, *Guildhall School of Music and Drama. Another production requiring specific period props. This time they were used constantly by the actors in a realistic setting.*
Photo: Laurence Burns

To liaise and communicate well a stage manager must make sure that their verbal and written skills are clear and articulate. Many a disaster has taken place through poor communication, costing some companies a lot of money. On one occasion a stage manager left written instructions to the props master to repair a large and expensive mechanical prop. Because the note was badly phrased, the prop was cut down in size making it useless; another had to be made at great speed therefore costing twice as much as the original.

You will need to forward plan very carefully, as this leads to the smooth running of the production period. Every play has its own special difficulties, so the ability to foresee clearly any potential obstacles and problems leads to a calmer, happier life for the stage management, the director, creative team and company.

The Deputy Stage Manager

DSM Qualities
- An understanding of the script
- An understanding of the director's and designer's interpretation of the production
- Passion for the job

- A love and understanding of people
- Caring
- Patience and tolerance
- Instinct
- Anticipation
- Assertiveness (not aggression)
- Ability to work as a team member
- Ability to work solo
- Not afraid of hard work and long hours
- Ability to give and take instruction
- Energy and tenacity
- Sense of humour
- Ability to laugh at yourself
- Awareness of others
- Methodical and systematic
- Good organizer
- Good communicator
- Good speaker
- Good listener
- Good note-taker
- Have an understanding of all things technical.

The title and role of the DSM is essentially British and relatively new, arriving some time in the 1960s when many new theatres were being built. New technology was being introduced, as well as a longer rehearsal time for the actors.

DSM Job

- Reading the play thoroughly
- Making notes of potential problems or difficult props and various priorities
- Making up the prompt copy
- Working closely with the SM on company and creative team contact
- Working closely with the SM on rehearsal room details, marking up and setting the room out with furniture and props
- Running daily rehearsals
- Dealing with the company and their needs
- Working closely with the SM team
- Contact with all the staging departments
- Keeping a check on the production progress
- Delegating tasks to the ASM/ASMs during the rehearsals
- Keeping all paperwork up to date making sure all changes are noted, particularly in the prompt copy
- Writing all setting and running lists, sound and Lx cues lists and wardrobe notes
- Keeping a clean, clear and efficient rehearsal room
- Attending all production meetings and sound and lighting sessions

- Putting all the cues into the prompt copy following the relevant designers' and the director's instructions
- Running the final run-throughs
- Making a list of the number of cue lights and headsets required and their best positions for the sound department
- Helping the SM team move from the rehearsal room to the theatre
- Attending a lighting session – this is often where cues get put into the script
- Assist in the setting up of the stage and wings for the technical rehearsal
- Helping to set up the prompt desk in a position suitable for cueing the show
- Attending all scene change rehearsals
- Running the cues from the prompt desk during the technical rehearsals
- Running the cues for the dress rehearsals, previews and press night
- Running all performances from the first night to the last
- Assist the SM team to put the show away at the end of the run

This created more work and opened up new departments within the theatre structure, creating a need for extra help for the poor overworked stage manager. In most other countries the position does not exist, the various jobs seem to be divided up between a stage manager, prompter and the director, resulting in a completely different approach to producing a show.

The DSM is deputy to the stage manager, responsible for running the rehearsal, prompting and taking notation of the actors' moves, and cueing the show in performance. However, an important part of their responsibilities is taking over the role of SM when necessary. One of the particular skills of the DSM is working closely with the director and the company of actors with patience, understanding, and gentle but firm discipline. The DSM must know and understand the play well. They must understand the designer's concept of the play and how the director is approaching the production. DSMs need to be aware of falling into the trap of concentrating on the mechanics of the production only and losing the other side of their role, which is to talk to the actors, listen to the ideas of the creative team and look into the writing of the play itself.

The DSM is responsible for making up the prompt copy; this becomes known as the 'Bible' and is a complete record of the production, containing every move, pause and action each

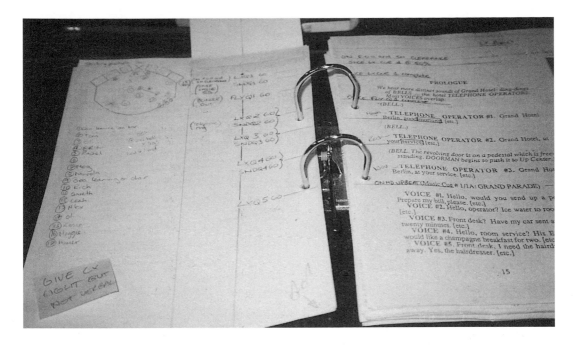

A completed prompt copy ready to cue the show with. This represents a great deal of work. It is also neat enough for another member of the team to use if necessary.

individual actor makes, plus details of all the technical cues and actors' calls to the stage.

This prompt copy never leaves the theatre except to be taken by the DSM each morning to the rehearsal room and returned each evening; it should never be taken home by anyone even the director! There are terrible but true stories of prompt copies being left on buses, at train stations and in restaurants, never to be seen again. In one case this meant making up a new copy at great speed; very tricky especially when it was only a few days before the opening night. To re-create detailed moves from day one of rehearsal up to the recently given cues is a difficult and upsetting task to perform.

Assistant Stage Manager

ASM Qualities
- Passion for the job
- Love of people
- Caring
- Patience and tolerance
- Understanding of people and their needs
- Ability to work as part of a team
- Ability to work solo
- Ability to take criticism
- Systematic and methodical
- Good organizer
- Neat and tidy worker
- Clear thinking
- Good note-taker
- Ability to take instruction
- An understanding of all things technical.

The ASM is an indispensable part of the team, who must have boundless energy, enjoy people and be utterly reliable. It is a fun position, with a good opportunity to find out all that is involved during the making of a production, an opportunity to experience and learn about the production process and make your own contribution to a successful show. Sometimes they are treated as the dogsbody of the team by bad stage managers,

ASM Job

- Reading the script thoroughly
- Making sure the design concept is understood
- Working closely with the SM team
- Communicating with the team on a daily basis
- Assisting in the marking out and setting up of the rehearsal room
- Attending rehearsals and making setting lists and notes with the DSM
- Making teas and coffees, running errands and answering the telephone in the rehearsal room
- Assisting in the keeping of a clean, clear and efficient rehearsal room
- Finding and borrowing props by telephone, on foot and exploring all antique and junk shops and local flea markets
- Making small props, such as scrolls and letters, period cigarette packets or flower bouquets
- Making lists
- Using the telephone, fax machine and photocopier, general office duties
- Shopping for small props, such as, notebooks, pens or fabric for covering cushions
- Attending some production meetings
- Assisting in the transfer from the rehearsal room to the theatre
- Assisting in the clearing and setting of the wings and stage for the lighting session
- Attending lighting sessions to walk the lights
- Running the wing or wings for the technical rehearsal
- Running the wing or wings for all dress rehearsals, previews and press nights
- Running the wings for all performances from the first to the last night
- Assisting in the putting away of the show after its run, and returning the borrowed and hired props

but thankfully there are few such stage managers in gainful employment.

The ASM's principal function is to assist the SM and DSM with the ongoing progress of the rehearsal and running of the production. A good stage manager will make the ASM feel a vital part of the team, by making sure they understand that whatever task is set them, it is an important part of the production process, whether it's cleaning and sweeping the stage, making teas and coffees, assisting with the organization of actors or attending fittings and calls. The many responsibilities of an ASM include finding and making props and servicing and setting them during rehearsals and performances.

THE DREAM TEAM

The sense of collaboration by stage management towards the same goal can be exciting with a strong sense of achievement on the first night. There has to be a good delegation of responsibilities, with everyone knowing what is happening and what to do . Care and commitment should be maintained throughout the rehearsal period and schedules and deadlines kept. One of the commandments of stage management is to learn when to supply, sometimes at a moment's notice, the shoulder to cry upon and that most necessary cup of tea to ease the problems and tensions. When stage management has made the production process clear and free from angst and stress for the director, company, creative team and staging departments alike, that's a dream team. When the audience and critics are unaware of the workings and activity backstage during a performance, and all they see is a well-presented and performed show, that's due to the dream team.

The dream team are stage management who are practical first-class organizers, enjoy working with people, and have a passion for the theatre. The dream team will be much sought after by managements and companies, and will always find themselves employed.

3 THE PLAY

The stage manager prepares for the first production of the season as soon as the play list has been announced. You should be like a personal assistant to the director managing, as the title implies, everything connected with the staging of the production. You will need to prepare, check, co-ordinate and list the props and furniture, take note of various stage settings, and allocate all necessary jobs to the rest of your team, ensuring that the total show comes together in time for the opening night.

Stage managers are usually excellent list-makers – the job is far too busy and varied to rely on memory alone however good the individual person's memory may be. The amount of paperwork that gathers while collating a show is enormous, and it is necessary to have information to hand at a moment's notice. The use of a computer, laptop and mobile phone, plus access to a fax machine, is extremely useful. However, there are times when all the modern conveniences in the world are not much use when you are called into the rehearsal room, and the director suddenly asks for the latest information on an actor's availability, or the new position and measurement of the door or window. To help a stage manager to have all the information at their fingertips, a simple portable filing system was born, the Production File.

THE PRODUCTION FILE AND CONTENT

The production file is the central nerve of the play's organization and collation and is carried by the stage manager everywhere they go during the rehearsal period. It is not closed and filed away for future reference until the show ends its run and the last prop has been returned. A vertical twin pocket folder is best, or if these are not available, you can stick two pocket folders back to back.

The production file will be a complete record of the show, allowing the production to be

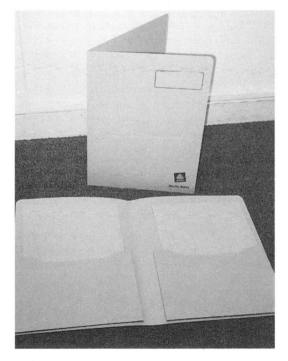

The making of a production file – twin-pocket folder.

reproduced in finite detail. It is a valuable record of a particular production that may be re-created to tour or transfer to London's West End. Perhaps a director needs to check details of an actor from a show that finished a year ago, or the stage manager needs to contact the furniture and prop hire firm to find a specific table or sofa used in a previous production.

The list of content will vary slightly with each production and will not be complete until the show has closed. Some shows are more complex than others; therefore one may need more or less information. Apart from the production file being the stage manager's mobile office, it is also a comprehensive record of the production for future

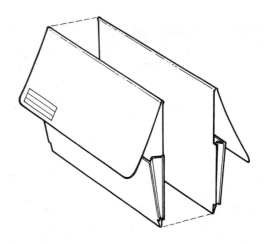

Two single pocket folders attached back to back.

Production File Content

Cast lists all dated and starting with the first one issued
All correspondence to and from the creative team and company
All correspondence to and from trade contacts, hire companies, production advisers, including faxes
Creative team list
Company and creative team contact sheets
Contact numbers for rehearsal rooms, props suppliers and trade companies
Rehearsal room details, booking confirmation letter including dates
Performance dates and times
Copies of all research material
Acquisitions chart
Scene availability chart
Actors non-availability chart
Programme details
Publicity information specifically for the company and this production
Complimentary tickets list and house seat allocation
Understudy or covers lists

Choreographer, dance and dancers' details if applicable
Wardrobe lists
All call sheets for all types of calls
Prop borrowing forms
Props breakdown lists
Rehearsal report sheets
Production meeting minutes and agendas
LX cue sheets
Sound cue sheets
Fly plot
Hanging plot
Dressing room list
Programme
Photographs of the set
Floppy disc of information
Curtain calls list
Crew allocation
Scene change list
Props setting list
Personal props list
Running list
Production schedule
Memos
Running times
Show report sheets

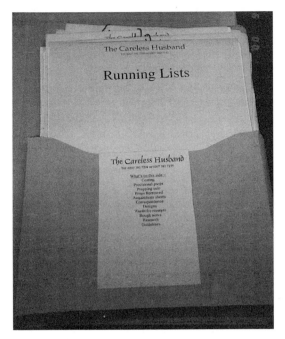

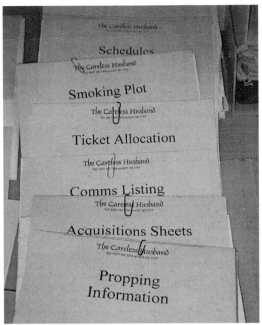

The production file and its contents. Note the list of contents on the front of the inner pocket.

The contents of a production file always contains these subjects except for the smoking plot that was an addition for this play.

reference. This becomes essential when touring or playing in repertoire, like the Royal National Theatre and Royal Shakespeare Company, Opera and Ballet companies, where a collection of shows are produced for a season, running for several weeks or perhaps months. The productions will alternate with each other throughout the season according to public demand.

READING THE PLAY

Becoming familiar with the play is the first most important part of stage management. You need to know the storyline very well and have an in-depth knowledge of the play in conjunction with the scenes, action and design. The design, when you acquire a copy of the play, may still be under discussion; however the original is often in plan or photographic form within the publication, and even the description in the stage directions will give you a guide as to the presentation. A lot of stage management think they can skim through the stage directions, but this does not give them the in-depth knowledge they require to really know their show. Read the play, and read it again. Let it soak into the brain. Know the work as closely as a car mechanic knows his car, a carpenter his wood or a conductor his score. At first you may not feel you understand the play at all; do not worry as the more you need to find out the more you learn. While reading the piece make notes from the text as this will help to make everything more familiar. You find out the period in which the play is set, the type of prop or piece of furniture the characters would have had in their house.

25

From this information you are able to build up a picture in your mind of these people and the author's storyline. This leads on to understanding why the director and designer insist on a certain style, colour or size of prop.

The director will often ask the stage management to research the period in which the play is set – for example if the play you were working on was *The Three Sisters* by Anton Chekhov you would be asked to find out about the lives of women in Russia in the late 1800s, what they ate, read, what they did for entertainment, and so on. There would be the need for information on Anton Chekhov – for example, when he wrote the play, how popular he was in his day, why he wrote the play. Then you would work your way through the prop list, finding out about Russian newspapers, luggage, glasses and bottles including any labels. All this reading and research will help to give the stage management the depth of knowledge it requires. The more you need to find out, the more you learn. Stage management must have a feel for the play, whether they are the DSM cueing the show or the SM collating the piece, or the ASM borrowing the correct prop. None of the knowledge and understanding of the theme, plot, background, climax and spectacle of the play will come to the stage management by just reading the stage directions and not the text, or only reading the play once.

Beware of stage management that has done the play before; it may think that it does not need to read it all again, sometimes not even opening the script. However, the script could be a different publication, with relevant sections cut or added. The designer and director will present it entirely differently and possibly update the period in which it is set, hence a new production.

The best way to assist your understanding and memory while reading through the text, and to serve as a good starting point for discussions at production meetings, is to make a production analysis chart. It is not a good thing to allow a designer or director to think that everything in

their script is possible technically and financially; if you can foresee potential problems that may crop up then you can help prevent a crisis.

PRODUCTION ANALYSIS CHART

The following is the type of problem a stage manager may find in a text. What do you do when during a scene in Act One a tray containing expensive bone china cups and saucers, silver tea pot, milk jug and sugar bowl, all filled with real tea, milk and sugar, is dropped as part of the play's action, but magically reappears in Act Two when the actors have a whole scene talking over their cups of tea from the same tea service? This of course would need quite a bit of discussion with the production manager and creative team, as there would be a number of implications concerning Health and Safety, with hot tea and broken china on the stage, possibly scalding or cutting the actors, budget concerns because this piece of stage business will make a mess of a hired or borrowed carpet or piece of furniture, not to mention having to replace a new expensive tea set for each performance. Then there might be a concern for the hired costumes, as tea and milk especially when mixed with sugar stain all fabrics. The costumes may not be washable because they are heavy brocade or fine silk. You should be looking for these types of problems when reading through a play.

The following is an illustration of one of the first pages of one of these charts from a play by Alan Ayckbourn called *Small Family Business*. This shows the Act/Scene/Page ... the Setting ... the Set Dressing ... the hand Props ... the Lx State and necessary FX ... the Sound FX... Various Wardrobe requirements. Within each of the squares of the graph are the stage manager's own comments about enquiries or concerns they may have at this point.

The first column is the page in the script where the technical requirement or prop appears. This will keep you on the same page

ct c: ge:	Stage Setting	Hand Props	Furniture and Dressings	Sound	Lx	Costume/ Wigs Specific Make-up	Notes
1-1	Composite set showing: bedroom, bathroom, kitchen, sitting room and hallway, with particular emphasis on doors – see notes	Briefcase containing £10,000 in tens, twenties and fifties	3 × seater sofa plus 3 cushions	car arrives and departs	Practical table lamps 2 × for sofa tables		All doors slammed continuously and hard. Bathroom has practical shower. A lot of action around bath
1-2	Kitchen – all units practical, plus kettle – cooker and fridge?	Washing-up liquid and bowl, plus squeezy dish mop	3 × stools and kitchen table – one chair	Two types of door bell and a chime			Appliances could be simulated or faked in some way – sink practical
1-2		Practical party food, lots of drinks, ice cubes and nibbles			Black eye at 3 stages, blood capsules. Blood: at least 2 bottles		Chicken drumsticks – pizza and trifle – bags of ice cubes from a supermarket!
1-3	Kitchen hallway. Sitting room	Sandwiches, 3 different telephones: 2 with long flex, 1 wall mounted		Different phone rings plus a trim phone		Pregnant padding, 7 months	All three areas used in the one scene, a lot of actions with phones – radio thrown
2.10		Briefcases numbers two and three – one with housing pamphlets from estate agent					money notes thrown from the bathroom platform over stage

A production analysis chart being put to good use.

with everyone else when you talk through the show. It will also clarify where the bulk of the potential problems will fall together with the various characters involved. Use the style of the following to use up less space on the page making it clear to see at a glance ... 1/2/6/ (which means it is Act One/Scene Two/page six). The second column is where the action takes place ... the Set ... the Dining Room of the Smith's House or the Inner Chamber of the Castle ... or the Battle of the Somme, etc. The next is Set Dressing ... the carpet or rugs/curtains/table lamps, and so on, of the Smith's

Dining Room, or an ornate carved chair for the Castle Inner Chamber, or pieces of warfare for the Battle of the Somme. Hand props ... the china or bowl of food the actor is carrying or handling in any way for the Smith's Dining Room, the scroll or large book for the actor in the Castle Inner Chamber, or rifle and pistol for the soldier in the Battle of the Somme.

As you read, you discover the actor's entrances and exits, their basic character descriptions, age and type of character, how they present themselves, whether they are wealthy or require make-up and costume changes between scenes

27

Points to Note about the Set

The stage manager should be aware of the following elements of the set:

Doors and windows and their location

Whether the actors and their props can get through the doors, particularly if they are wearing large hats or wide crinolines

If any part of the stage will be raked (the stage floor sloping towards the audience) and a wheelchair or pram is used in the play

Any trap doors in the stage

If there are trucks to be pushed on and off stage by the actors or with actors on them

Flying pieces that come in and out during the action

Curtains or blinds pulled by actors

Any naked flames such as candles or campfires.

Any form of pyrotechnics

and acts; and whether the characters have to fight, fall or roll on the stage floor. Perhaps they need pockets in their costumes, require a watch, handkerchief or pair of spectacles as this could be an issue for the wardrobe department. The chart shows the time of year, month, day and any specific notes for the lighting designers; perhaps outside, it's night-time with a full moon, or early morning with the sun shining, or it may be raining, or there may be a street lamp. Inside, perhaps the curtains are closed, a table lamp is on with a cosy log fire burning in the grate. The sound department would need to know the details of the traffic noises or birds singing, distant gunfire, radio announcers or music.

ACQUISITIONS CHART

Having read the play thoroughly and made the above analysis chart you would now be able to make a stage management Acquisition Chart. This chart is laid out in a similar way to the play analysis, except it tells you where you have acquired your items from, plus the various contacts, collection and return dates.

This chart is invaluable to stage management enabling it to keep a daily update on the collation of the show in finite detail. It is also invaluable when setting up scenes in rehearsal and for pro-

viding information about the personal props an actor may need to take along to a wardrobe fitting to check the size of the pocket required in their costume, or whether the specs are suitable.

PLANNING THE OFFICE AND KEEPING IT TIDY

Much of the work is hands on for stage management with a lot of travelling between the rehearsal room and the theatre where your base is. At your base there would be an office allocated to the team from where all lists and charts are drawn up, telephone calls and stage management team meetings take place. This office must be kept clear and tidy and used only as an office with a lockable desk, cupboard or filing cabinet and not used as a green room. There also is a tendency for the team to use the office space as a prop store. As everything is found or bought, so it goes into a corner of the office and gradually the items take over and there is no room for the stage manager and indeed the team. Always try to find another space or cupboard elsewhere in the theatre to store items and if the prop is not too valuable or fragile, it should go into rehearsal as you acquire it. Any valuable props should be stored in the production manager's safe, size permitting. A neat well-ordered office shows a high

Cn/	Item	Stock	Make	Buy	Hire	Borrow	Donate	Collect/ rtn	Notes
1-1	Market stall green-grocery		Workshop to make						Stall to double as backing for the Somme and recruitment office
1-1	Dummy produce for above	Prop room	Borrow and make (Jeff)						Check what 's in season and no foreign produce!
1-1	2 boxes real apples and carrots			Local market, Don's stall (Judy)					Try for a donation from the market
1-1	Oil lamp, storm lantern	Prop room or Lx dept							Able to suspend; mime blowing it out and lighting it, and to dim to out for end of scenes
1-1	Black iron scales					Mrs Cooper Arts Antiques, 26 High Street 0172 5806		Collect 21.9.01 (Jeff) return 7.11.01	Practical must have weights
1-2	Enamel jug and tea			Buy tea and milk (sugar not seen)		Try to borrow: scouts or pensioners		Collect 17.9.01 (Judy) return 7.11.01	Preferably brown in colour. Now found scouts
1-2	2 white enamel mugs			Kitchen shop High Street 99p each					
1-2	Squares of blackboard and chalk		6 boards 10" × 9"				chalk donated by H. Parkard	posting to us 20.9.01	For prices of goods chalk to rewrite the prices

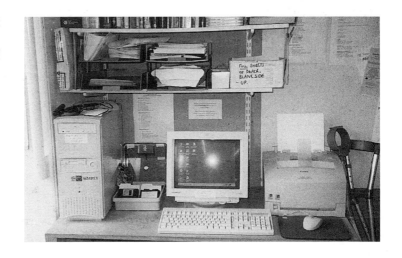

(Above) Acquisitions chart for Accrington Pals. *These charts are filled in by hand as they can constantly change.*

A neat and tidy office makes it much easier to work.

Lists and charts are easily accessible on a large notice-board in a prominent position in the office.

standard of efficiency. It generally means the stage manager is clear thinking and on the ball. A well-laid-out notice board with daily information such as call sheets, acquisition charts, individual work sheets, and a good-sized wall diary are invaluable aids. Various prop contact names and numbers would also be displayed on the board for easy access.

Make sure all the company's personal phone numbers are safely in your production file, never have them pinned to the notice board for obvious security reasons. Sometimes sensitive material such as faxes, e-mails and private notes may be accessible in the office, which is another reason why it should not be used as a green room. The contact sheet is another importantly laid out piece of paper.

A contact sheet is valuable information if the next day's rehearsal call or venue have changed, especially if you have not seen the actor concerned because they were not called to rehearse on a particular day.

A contact sheet for an actor. This would be included in the welcome pack sent to them before rehearsals started.

COMPANY CONTACT SHEET   'ALFIE'

NAME   --
PERM. ADDRESS   --

TELEPHONE NO: --

LOCAL ADDRESS   --

TELEPHONE NO: --

AGENTS ADDRESS   ---

TELEPHONE NO: --
MOBILE   ---
FAX   --
E-MAIL   ---
OTHER   --

GENERAL NOTES   --

----

4 PRE-PRODUCTION

As soon as the season has been decided on and announced, a good stage manager starts to think about the problems ahead. We have already discussed the importance of knowing your play and the experienced stage manager will know that any Ayckbourn requires a lot of props, a pantomime will have a large cast or a Shakespeare will include a fight scene. At this point a particular play may not be very familiar to you, but as you become knowledgeable about different authors you will become more aware of the general problems associated with staging any particular play.

Knowing the problems will trigger a host of questions and the first opportunity to answer these questions is at the white card meeting. This is the first time the production staff see the model of the design. It is called a white card meeting because that is exactly how the model will be presented, as an unpainted white card with no colour details and only the main features represented. The purpose of the meeting is to present a general idea and to discuss some of the major staging aspects of the production. The director and the designer will have discussed the way in which the play is to be presented, they will be aware of the budget, the physical limitations of the theatre and the number of staff available to work on the production. The production manager will have provided much of this information and at the meeting the director and designer will present their ideas for the production, based upon this information.

All the heads of the staging departments will be present and they will be looking at the model from their particular point of view. The construction manager will want to know the materials that the designer wants to use. How will the larger pieces of scenery be used, will they be flown or built as a truck that is moved around the stage? The wardrobe supervisor will want to know how many costumes each character will have and if any characters have been cut. The props department will need a list of props to be made and which ones are practical working props and which can be dummies. The director and designer will have thought about many of these questions and will be ready to answer them during the meeting and the answers should be readily available to the various departments.

Stage management are in a different position from the other staging departments because the process that affects them most has not yet started. This meeting will take place before rehearsals have started. Stage management will have a provisional props list from the script but the list will not be complete until the rehearsals are over. Some props in the list will not be required while the director and designer will add others as the rehearsal progresses. It is impossible to know at this stage all the props that will be required. This makes it very difficult to judge how much money you will need to provide the props. The questions you need to ask at the white card meeting include confirmation that any unusual or expensive props are likely to be required, if any food mentioned in the script will be real or not and if any of it will be eaten.

A good production manager will leave the director and designer to allocate the money according to their artistic priorities. He will advise them about any special conditions unique to his theatre, which may involve extra cost and will provide a budget divided between the departments but will leave the detailed decisions to the creative team. At the white card meeting the director and designer will present their ideal production, the heads of the staging departments will then work out the cost of providing this ideal, which is known as the costing process. Inevitably the cost will come to more than the production budget. It is then up to the director and designer to make the necessary changes to bring the costs within the budget. The production manager will guide the creative team through this process and will be responsible for making sure that the show remains within budget. It is very important that all the staging departments keep within their individual budgets and that overall the production does not cost any more than the budget allows. Theatre companies today have very tight finances and if one production goes over budget it means that another production later on in the season may not have as much money to spend.

REHEARSAL ROOMS

The play has been decided on, the design presented, the cast chosen and the rehearsals are about to start. Before they begin, the stage manager needs to book a rehearsal room. Sometimes it is possible to rehearse in a space within the theatre, perhaps the studio theatre is free or it is the first production of the season and the stage is clear. If it is possible to rehearse within your base theatre this will save the company money and make your life much easier during the rehearsal period. Much of the time, however, rehearsals have to take place outside the theatre and one of your most important tasks will be to choose and book a suitable rehearsal space.

The ideal rehearsal room simply does not exist but there are various facilities that will make the whole rehearsal process smoother if they are available. When looking for rehearsal space you should consider the following:

- Is the space large enough or of similar proportions to the theatre stage?
- How accessible is the space for both the company and the theatre van delivering props and furniture?
- Does it have facilities such as a kitchen, loos and public telephone?
- Is it adequately heated or ventilated depending upon the time of year?
- Would the company have exclusive use of the premise or do others share it, particularly in the evenings and at weekends?
- Are there any restrictions on the use of the facilities, such as no marking tape on the floor or notices pinned to the walls?
- Is there any natural light and if so can this be blacked out if necessary?
- Are there any additional side rooms or smaller rooms available, which could be used by the company?
- Are there good surrounding facilities such as a nearby café or pub, shops, banks and public transport?

The reasons why these aspects are important are discussed in detail in Chapter 9.

CONTACTING THE COMPANY AND THE CREATIVE TEAM

Before rehearsals start you should contact the company and the creative team. Your theatre management will have been in touch with the actors via their agents to negotiate their contract but now is the point when you as their stage manager need to make contact.

The first person to contact is the director who will by now have an idea of what they wish to do on the first day of rehearsals. Sometimes the director will want to read the play

A clear, clean rehearsal room ready for action.

through with the entire cast or they may wish to work with the principals for the first few days. Once you have introduced yourself to the director, usually by telephone, you will have a better idea of how they wish to run the rehearsal period. The information you need from the director includes whether or not they wish to have a mark-up from the first day or would rather see the space for themselves before deciding which way round in the room they wish to sit. You will also want to find out what time rehearsals will start, particularly on the first day. Rehearsals usually start at 10:00am but on the first day this may be later to allow the company to travel from their permanent home to the theatre.

You are now able to write to the rest of the creative team and the company to introduce yourself and to let them know the call for the first day of rehearsal. The time and date an actor is required in rehearsal is referred to as the call and this varies on a daily basis, sometimes more often. Included in your letter should be directions to the rehearsal room and the theatre if these are two different places, and information about the theatre and its staff as well as general local information such as bus services, local restaurants and bed and breakfast accommodation. Many theatres have a list of local landlords who provide accommodation for actors visiting the theatre and this list should be included in your introductory letter.

The Contents of the Actors' Welcome Letter and Information Pack

Welcome letter
Script
Map of the area marking the theatre and the rehearsal room, parking and public transport, banks, shops, pubs and cafés
Map of the inside of the theatre
List of staff
Cast list
Accommodation list
Blank contact sheet to fill in
Blank wardrobe measurement form
Request for a photograph and the actor's biography for the programme
Request for salary payment details for the accounts department

The wardrobe measurement form asks for actor's basic measurements, the wardrobe department always checks these later but they give an indication of an actor's size. There will be a request from the marketing department for an actor's biography and photograph that will be used for publicity purposes and printed in the programme later. Some theatres have a house style for actors' biographies but the marketing and publicity department will still require the basic details as soon as possible. Actors' agents are another source for a biography and some actors refer the marketing department directly to their agents. An actor's wages are also sometimes paid directly to their agent. If this is not the case a form requesting details of the actor's bank account in order that their wages can be paid directly should also be included in this letter. As the stage manager, you will need to know about any allergies, particularly food allergies, the company may have as there is nearly always food of some kind required in a play. Finally you would include a contact sheet for the actor to complete and this should include all possible contact numbers at which the actor can be reached as well as the address of their digs and permanent home address.

THE FIRST PRODUCTION MEETING

The first production meeting is one of the most important meetings. It is at this point that the artistic compromises have to be made. The director and designer have presented their ideas and the staging departments have established how much it will cost to produce. Inevitably the cost of this ideal production will exceed the budget available. At the first production meeting the production manager must steer the director and designer through the process of cutting some elements of the production in order to bring the overall cost within the budget.

The director and designer will have seen the costings before attending this meeting and will have had an opportunity to discuss which elements of the production they wish to cut. The staging departments can be a great help in suggesting cheaper alternatives for an expensive prop, elaborate costume or specialized lighting effect. All the staging departments should be as positive as possible during this process. It is much better to offer cheaper alternatives than to take an 'it's too expensive therefore it's cut' attitude. The creative team may accept an alternative or they may decide to cut some elements altogether in order to keep an effect, costume or special prop which they consider more important to the overall production. These decisions should be the creative team's prerogative, supported by the production manager and accurate and comprehensive information from the staging departments.

PAGES 35–39
A costing sheet for a production of **David Copperfield**.

'David Copperfield'	Estimated Production Budget		Production
SUMMARY		PAINT	£123.21
		Technical	£14,148.12
		Props/SM	£2,199.98
		WARDROBE	£4,558.00
		LX	£1,045.00
		SOUND	£3,900.00
		TOTAL	£25,974.31
		BUDGET	£30,000.00
		OVER/UNDER	−£4,025.69

PAINT	ITEM		COST
	white	7.5 litres	£24.41
	black	3 × 5 litres	£54.06
	Krylon gold spray	400ml	£4.65
	spectrum red	½ litre	£8.90
	burnt umber	½ litre	£8.90
	raw sienna	½ litre	£8.90
	Hycote fluorescent	200ml	£2.50
	masking tape	6 × ½in rolls	£3.00
	Hammerite	½ litre	£6.90
	white spirit	1 litre	£0.99
PAINT TOTAL			£123.21

TECHNICAL MAN.	ITEM	QUANTITY	COST
White Arch	18mm ply 8 x 4 sheet	3 sheets	£44.61
	White Canvas	8m	£39.36
	front pros total	**£83.97**	
Ballet Floor	flooring	2 × 25m rolls	£1,200.00
	Tape		
Tab Tracks	Tab Track	3	£2,509.50
White wipe	Sheeting		£123.89
Black wipe 1	Serge	5 × 6m	£265.74
Black wipe 2	Serge	5 × 6m	£265.74
	Additional costs		£80.00
	Total wipe costs	**£735.37**	
Fire Place	18mm ply 8 × 4 sheet	2	£29.74
	Black serge	2m	£11.06
	Total Fire Place	**£40.80**	
Table Truck	18mm ply 8 × 4 sheet	3	£44.61
	Castors	12	Stock
	12m ply	1	£20.00
	1 × 1 steel	24m	£15.60
	Table Truck total	**£80.21**	
4 Door Frames	40 × 40 box steel	24m	£44.64
	Castors	16	£6.80
	Sill Irons	4 × 1m	Stock
	Door Frame total	**£51.44**	
Screen Frame	1 × 1 × 1.5mm box steel	42m	£27.30

Estimated Production Budget *continued*

	Castors		4	£3.40
	Canvas	3m		£14.76
	Total Screen Frame		**£45.46**	
Small Table	18mm ply 8 × 4 sheet		1	£14.87
	Castors		4	£3.40
Swing	To be designed	Global		£100.00
Tempest Cloth	Whaleys	6 × 4m		£95.52
Star Cloth	Fibre optics		2	£9,000.00
Treads	18mm ply 8 × 4 sheet		2	£29.74
	4mm ply 8 × 4 sheet		1	£7.84
Steel Deck	8 × 4		4	stock
	1m legs		24	stock
	Serge	10m		stock
Dye lines		Global		£50.00
Fixings				£100.00
Technical Management Total				**£14,148.12**

PROPS/SM

	Knitting needles			£7.00
	Wool Skein			£20.00
	paper hats			£50.00
	Gladstone bag			£40.00
	bottles of wine			stock
	Alka seltzer		3	£5.67
	glass			stock
	napkin			Stock
	badminton rackets and cock			£20.00
Dogs	stiff feather boa			£7.00
	glove puppet			£2.00
	letters			stock
	camera			£35.00
	flash	3 × £1.70		£5.10
	chair			stock
	rule			stock
	3 handkerchiefs			stock
	large playing cards			£6.00
	2 life buoys			borrow
	fob watch chains		2	£32.00
	burnt food on plate			£10.00
	wedding bouquet			£20.00
	bentwood chairs		4	stock
	butterfly net			£4.00
	helium balloon heart			£10.00

	streamers		£20.00
	petal drop		£25.00
	plastic plates	6	£20.00
	flowers for rope		£20.00
	Victorian shed	hire	£150.00
	Victorian wheel chair	hire	£250.00
	Sundries		£100.00
	Table cloth		£16.00
Footlights × 13	Plaster and scrim		£5.00
	resin and fibre glass		£41.00
	pigment		£2.00
	ply base		stock
	total footlights	**£48.00**	
seagulls	nylon monofilament		£4.00
	ply		stock
	labour		£60.00
Umpires chair	Box steel 125 × 125		£25.50
	Castors		£28.80
	timber set and dressing		£20.00
	LABOUR		£300.00
Birds	steel wire		£40.00
	prop canaries	4	£30.00
	butterflies	5	£10.00
Kangaroo	18mm ply 8 × 4 sheet	1	£14.87
boat	18mm ply 8 × 4 sheet	1	£14.87
Case	9mm ply	1	£31.00
	fabric		£15.00
Chaise	Fabric braid		£20.00
Coffee cup	fibre glass & resin		£10.00
Kite	bamboo		£2.00
	fabric		£10.00
Cookery book	polystyrene		£0.00
lawyers	wig stands	4	£19.80
	12mm plastazote	1	£18.50
	½" foam	1 sheet	£2.00
	labour		£300.00
Kids	foam		£23.00
	fabric		£15.00
	habad & glue		£25.00
	labour		£200.00
Small kangas	18mm ply 8 × 4 sheet	1	£14.87
masks		6	£30.00
PROPS /SM TOTAL			**£2,199.98**

WARDROBE			
Character	**ITEM**	**SOURCE**	**COST**
Dave	2 outfits & frockcoat	hire	£250.00
	trousers	buy	£50.00
	top hat	make	£50.00
	shoes	buy	£80.00

	Estimated Production Budget *continued*		
Mr Dick	2 outfits and jackets	hire	£250.00
	leggings	buy	£50.00
	wig	buy	£30.00
pegotty	chunky jumper	buy	£50.00
Sterforth	fitted	buy	£33.00
	shoes	buy	£33.00
	top hat	make	£50.00
priest	robes	find	
	shoes	find	
	hat	find	
Mr Macawber	trousers	buy	£50.00
	shirt	buy	£40.00
	shoes	buy	£70.00
	top hat	make	£50.00
	waist coat	hire	£80.00
	padding	find	
Traddles	top hat		
	basic outfit	global	£100.00
Heep	jacket	hire	£250.00
	shirt	buy	£40.00
	leggings	buy	£25.00
Ham	as Heep & trimmings		£100.00
Wickfield	Basic outfit & top hat		£100.00
Littimer	as Wickfield		£100.00
Betsy	corset	buy	£100.00
	leotard	buy	£70.00
	crinoline	make	£120.00
	trimmings	buy	£25.00
	shoe coat bonnet	find	
Miss Noel	as Betsy		
	hat	find	
Agnes	corset	buy	£50.00
	leotard	buy	£50.00
	crinoline	make	£120.00
	trimmings		£30.00
	shoes & hat	find	
Dora	crinoline	make	£60.00
	underskirt	make	£50.00
	corset	buy	£50.00
	white leotard	buy	£70.00
	trimmings	buy	£30.00
	veil	make	£25.00
	wig	buy	£80.00
	shoes & hat	find	
Emily	as Dora		
	trimmings	buy	£25.00
	hat	find	
	skirt	make	£40.00
Miss Steerforth	as Mrs Macawber		

	shoes	find		
	trimmings	buy		
	hat	make		
	Global figure			£85.00
Mr Spenlow	hat	make		£50.00
	leggings	buy		£50.00
	waistcoat	find		
	shirt	buy		£40.00
	jacket	hire		£250.00
	shoes	find		
	wig	hire		£200.00
Mrs Macawber	corset	buy		£50.00
	leotard	buy		£70.00
	crinoline	make		£60.00
	shoes apron cap	find		
	babies	make		£50.00
Rosa Dartle	corset	buy		£100.00
	leotard	buy		£80.00
	crinoline	make		£120.00
	shoes	find		
	trimmings	buy		£30.00
Mrs Heep	as Rosa			
	trimmings	buy		£25.00
Mrs Macawber	bonnet	find		
	small skirt	find		
	top layer	find		
Beggar		find		
Mrs Murdstone		Global		£25.00
Lavinia & Clarissa		find		
GLOBALS	insoles / laces			£50.00
	dry cleaning bill			£30.00
	hair / make-up			£200.00
	tights stockings			£100.00
WARDROBE TOTAL				**£4,558.00**

LX	ITEM			COST
Fireside Flicker	Motors		2	£180.00
	discs		2	£70.00
	fan		1	£20.00
Bubblemachine	hire	3 weeks		£60.00
Gel & gobos	global			£200.00
dry ice	machine	3 weeks		£75.00
	ice			£600.00
	fan			£20.00
LX TOTAL				**£1,045.00**

SOUND	ITEM			COST
musicians	per session = £50.00 per person		23	£3,450.00
studio		3 sessions		£350.00
audio formats				£100.00
SOUND TOTAL				**£3,900.00**

The meeting can become quite tense and it can take some time to resolve all the conflicts between the ideal production and the affordable one. The staging departments must not allow themselves to be persuaded to produce something more cheaply than they have costed to do. Pressure is often put upon the departments to provide the same elements for less money. This is particularly true of the stage management who are usually asked by the designer 'can't we borrow it?' This may be possible but cannot be guaranteed, and whilst the designer may be optimistic about this it is wise for you to take a more cautious view.

It is important that members of each department sit together at this meeting – this helps the production manager to address each department in turn and provides an opportunity for any private conversations that may be necessary during the meeting. It is part of your responsibility as the stage manager to set up a room for this meeting. Nameplates should be provided giving the name of each person present along with their title and department if applicable. A table around which everyone can sit is essential as some departments will have a lot of information such as brochures, sample books and price lists to present. The model and all its elements should also be on display, as it may need to be referred to.

You must take the opportunity at this meeting to clarify any questions that you have at this stage of the production. The first production meeting may well occur before the rehearsals have started and therefore many of the issues that stage management will need to resolve have not yet occurred. There will still be many questions for you to ask and they will include questions relating to the following:

- If there is fighting in the script does the director intend to include this, and if so how many weapons and of what type will be required?
- Will any food mentioned in the script be required and can the director confirm if it is to be eaten or not?
- Which of the alternative cheaper props would the director like or do they wish to cut something else in order to afford the original idea?
- Are there enough stage management and crew to carry out the scene changes as they are scripted or described by the designer, and if not to flag this up for the attention of the production manager?

It is impossible to document all the possible questions a stage manager may ask at this production meeting. If you follow the rule that any question should be asked as soon as possible and that as a stage manager you will actively seek information rather than take a wait-and-see approach, then you will be able to compile your own list according to the play and style of production in which you are involved.

5   THE REHEARSAL PERIOD – THE FIRST DAY

The first day of rehearsals is always a very exciting day. A new group of creative people are starting a process, that in a few short weeks will result in a new production to entertain thousands of people. It is important that this first day runs smoothly, and as the stage manager you play an important role in ensuring that the rehearsal period starts off positively.

With this in mind the whole stage management team should be available to attend rehearsal on the first day. A useful way to approach the day is to think of yourself as the host or ambassador for your theatre. A large proportion of the people arriving will be new to the theatre and probably to your town as well.

Even if your artistic director is directing the play and a large number of the cast have worked at the theatre before, there will be quite a few who have not. Remember this combination of cast and creative team have not worked together as a company before and you and your team are some of the few people who know who they all are.

You and your team will need to arrive at least an hour and a half before you expect anyone else to. You will need to prepare the rehearsal room for the day and to an extent for the rest of the rehearsal period. Having discussed with the director which way round they wish to use the room, you and the team can mark the set out on the rehearsal room floor.

Preparing for the mark-out. The rehearsal room needs to be as clear as possible before you start.

THE MARK-OUT

The mark-out is the process by which the set, represented on the ground plan, is re-created on the rehearsal room floor to its actual size. Ground plans are drawn by the designer and show an illustration of the set twenty-five times smaller than reality. This means that for every 1cm drawn on the ground plan the actual size will be 25cm on the stage. For every 10cm on the ground plan there will be 250cm on the stage. This is represented by 1:25cm written in the bottom right-hand corner of the plan. Most theatre designers follow this convention and draw to this scale. You can buy a scale ruler from a good quality stationers – this makes the measuring of the ground plan much easier as the maths is done for you.

Once you have made sure you have chosen the right scale, scale rulers provide six different scales; according to the one marked on the ground plan you can then read off from the ruler and measure straight on to the rehearsal room floor. If, using the scale ruler, a line on the ground plan measures one, then one metre should be measured on the floor. Rehearsal rooms are very rarely the same size and shape as your stage and one of the first decisions you will have to make is where to place the mark-up in the rehearsal room to provide the maximum amount of space to represent the set. There are other factors to be taken into consideration that are discussed fully in Chapter 9, but marking out as much of the set as possible is certainly one of your main priorities.

You will not be able to represent all the elements of the set and you will have to choose which areas you will leave out. The first areas to be sacrificed will be those not included in the acting area. The ground plan will represent all the designer's set including the pretty bits at the side that are there for atmosphere and will never be stepped upon by an actor. There is rarely space in a rehearsal room to represent

Starting the mark-out.

these areas. Your rehearsal room may not be large enough for the whole set area but it must be large enough for you to mark out at the very least the acting area of the set.

There are two very important lines drawn on all ground plans. One is called the setting line and the other the centre line. The centre line is drawn down the centre of the stage and the setting line denotes the edge of the designed area. There are two ways of marking out a set in a rehearsal room. The first method involves measuring the position of a point on the set by how far up the centre line and how far out from the centre line it is. The other method is sometimes referred to as arcing. This involves the use of two fixed points on the ground plan. Commonly the onstage edges of the proscenium arch would be used, but they can be any two fixed points as long as they are downstage left and right of the main acting area. Measurements are taken from these two fixed points directly to a point on the ground plan. This gives two measurements rather like a set of co-ordinates. You need to establish where in the rehearsal room your two fixed points from the ground plan are. Then fix a tape measure to each of these fixed points. Find the left-hand measurement on the left-hand

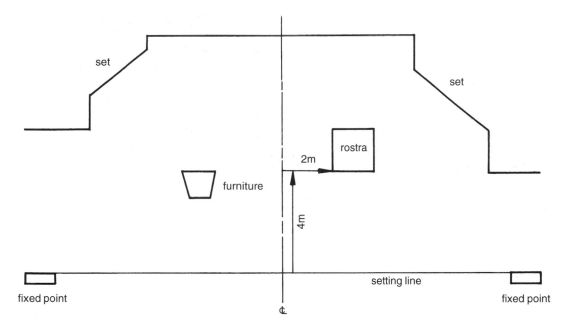

Marking out using the centre line and measuring out.

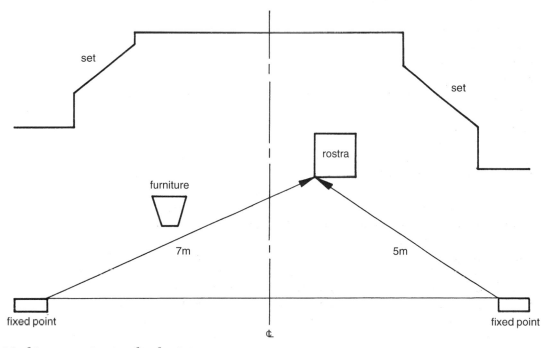

Marking out using two fixed points.

tape and the right on the right-hand tape. The point at which these two measurements meet is the point on the rehearsal room floor where the point on the ground plan will actually be.

It is a good idea to annotate your ground plan before you arrive at the rehearsal room to start your mark-out. The first task is to establish where in the rehearsal room the setting and centre lines will actually be. Then using either or both of the methods described above and following the measurements you have already written on your ground plan you and your team can complete the mark-out. Ideally, coloured PVC tape should be used to create the lines on the floor. A different colour can be used for each scene or act but be careful not to allow a complicated set to look like a scrambled underground map!

The director can help you decide which elements of the set should be marked up. Some directors require only the main shape of the set to be re-created. On other occasions it may be more important to mark a section of the set in detail with only an outline of the main set. It is important to remember when making these compromises what the purpose of a mark-out is. It is to give the actors and director an accurate map of the set in the rehearsal room. The DSM during rehearsals should remind the company of the limitations of the set as represented by the mark-up. If the company rehearses their moves, entrances, and if applicable, the choreography according to the mark-out, there will be fewer surprises when the company transfer to the actual set.

As you become more experienced with mark-outs they will become easier and the compromises and decisions forced upon you by the lack of space in the rehearsal room will be more straightforward. However, even a simple mark-out can take a couple of hours. If possible it is a good idea to gain access to the rehearsal room the day before rehearsals begin so that you can complete the mark-out without the pressure of the first day.

OTHER PREPARATIONS

As well as completing the mark-out you need to set up the room ready for the read-through of the play if this is what the director wishes to do on the first day. Usually the entire acting company are called and the designer, costume designer, if you have one, and occasionally the lighting designer will also attend. In addition to you and your team the heads of the staging departments will also be present. This gives the acting company an opportunity to meet such people as the wardrobe supervisor, scenic

Marking-Out Equipment

PVC tape of various colours
    approximately 1cm wide
Ground plan with the
    measurements already
    marked
Scale ruler
Two cloth measuring tapes
    preferably 25 metres or longer
Pencils and erasers
Notepad

(Above) Section of a completed mark-out.

Section of a completed mark-out showing the direction of steps.

artist, construction manager and chief electrician who are as crucial to the final production as they and the stage management team are. When setting up the room you need to provide enough chairs for all of these people and a table for the designer's model with an anglepoise lamp to light the model box. You may also need to provide notice-boards or flip charts for various research articles, a storyboard and the costume designs to be displayed. These should be arranged in such a way that everyone seated can easily see the model and anything else the designer wishes to present.

A very important ingredient on this first day is plenty of tea and coffee, preferably supplemented by a large box of biscuits. It's a good idea to have herbal or fruit teas, decaffeinated coffee and fruit juice available as well. It is customary for this to be free on the first day but during the rehearsal period, depending on the view of your management, there may be a small charge for tea and coffee. Once you have completed the mark-up, laid out the chairs, set up any necessary tables, unpacked the tea and coffee and boiled the kettle, you are ready to start the day!

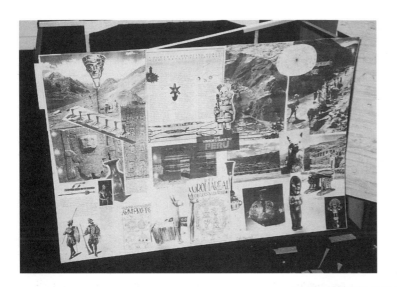

Research storyboard for **Royal Hunt of the Sun.**

(Below) Example of a costume design and material details that may be on view during the read-through; this costume was for **Royal Hunt of the Sun.**

THE REST OF THE DAY

As soon as the first person nervously peeps through the rehearsal room door, you as the stage manager will be occupied with welcoming the company. Introductions need to be made, coffee and tea provided, questions answered and problems solved. Actors have been known to arrive without enough change to pay the taxi still waiting outside, or they may wish to book into their digs and need directions quickly in order to make it back in time for the call.

If the company is called for 10:00am you can be sure there will be an early bird turning up at 9:30am, probably with a problem. Many actors turn up without some vital piece of paper. You should have spare copies of all the paperwork you sent out with the welcoming pack. There should also be spare copies of the script for those who have left them on the train, in the office or back at their digs. It is impossible to detail here all the problems and questions you may encounter on the first morning. As a good stage manager you should be prepared for as many as you can think of and react positively to those that take you by surprise. Experience will teach you to expect almost anything and one of the many challenges

of your job is meeting the situation with a smile and solving the query to the best of your ability.

As well as the creative team, company and production staff there will be a few other members of

Digs

A word of warning about actors and their digs! This can be a very sensitive area and it is advisable never to personally book accommodation for an actor if you can avoid it. You must certainly provide the information but individual preferences are so different that it is much better if actors choose their own accommodation.

staff present at this first rehearsal. These will include the marketing manager or press and publicity staff, the business manager representing your theatre's management and sometimes the author of the play. It is useful for the company to know who these people are and in turn they may have specific questions for the company.

The whole stage management team have a part to play in the smooth running of the day. Whilst the whole team need to introduce themselves to the arriving company, it is useful to allocate specific tasks to your DSM and ASM. For instance the DSM should make sure that everybody has the correct script and is clear about the plans for the day. They may also be responsible for collecting all those forms sent out in the welcome pack. Hopefully these are now all completed with the correct information. The ASM should be put in charge of the tea and coffee. This gives a possibly inexperienced member of the team one task to focus on and ensures that even the shyest ASM will automatically meet nearly everyone present. The DSM will already have made up the prompt copy including any cuts to the script that are already known. The director may give more cuts immediately before the read-through and the DSM should update the prompt copy accordingly.

There is no definitive list of duties for each member of the stage management team. The stage manager should be the first point of contact for the company and the director; the DSM's prime responsibility is anything to do with the details of the day or any future rehearsals and the ASM needs to watch, listen and learn and follow the stage manager's instructions. If the stage management are seen to be professional, confident in their roles and working well as a team they will have done much to set a positive tone for the day. This in turn will give the company confidence that they are in safe hands and will contribute greatly to a successful rehearsal period.

Generally, after the introductions and coffee have been completed the director will invite everyone to sit and listen to the creative team's presentation about the production. This can take some time but valuable details will be learnt at this point. You and your team must take exhaustive notes during this briefing to be compared later. If each member of the team takes his or her own notes there is less chance of the team as a whole missing an important point. This briefing will probably take until lunchtime when you will be asked where the best pub is or the cheapest café. After lunch the briefing may continue or the read-through will start. Not all of those present in the morning will stay for the read-through. The marketing manager and business manager may return to the theatre and the heads of department may be too busy working on the current production or the next one to stay for the whole afternoon.

After the read-through the DSM needs to be sure they know the call for the next day and you need to make sure that this is typed up and posted on all the relevant notice-boards after of course making sure that any actors dashing out of the rehearsal room know the next day's call. Once you are sure that all notes from the day have been collated and any requiring immediate action have been dealt with, you and your team can go home. That is of course providing you are not needed for the evening performance of the current show!

Stage manager's compartmentalized equipment box.

Suggested Contents of a Stage Management Equipment Box

Small torch

Multipurpose tool such as a penknife but with screwdriver, scissors, file, pliers and any other combination of implements

Small stapler

Hole punch

Self-adhesive tape

Drawing pins

Paper clips

Sticky notes

Spare rolls of PVC tape

String

Small domestic tape measure

Long surveyor's type tape measure for marking up

Scale ruler

Metric rule

Spare blank paper

Small envelopes

Calculator

Spare batteries for any other equipment used

Phone card or small amount of telephone change

Anything else you need for your particular production or that you think may be useful!

6 THE REHEARSAL PERIOD

The rehearsal progress of any show is a period of constant discovery, change and improvement. There is a pattern in the progress lasting approximately four weeks, starting with a reading of the text by the company followed by discussions with the director. There will be various sessions of experimentation and improvisation in which the actors find their characterization. Then the director starts to move the actors around the set, commonly known as blocking. You and your team will have dealt with all pre-planning, have a prepared prompt script, all relevant paperwork in the production file and have been to the first rehearsal. The whole team are now responsible for keeping track of any changes and developments throughout the rehearsal process and continue to be a source of help and support for the company and creative team.

A Typical Rehearsal Period

Read-through
Blocking
Prompting
Stagger-through
Run through
Transferring from rehearsal room to the
    stage

READ-THROUGH

For the read-through of a straight play, the stage management would set up the room with tables and chairs, having discussed with the director the most suitable layout. This could be in the form of either of the diagrams overleaf. If you were in a read or sing-through the most likely layout would be a circle or in groups.

As well as your standard equipment you will need a large supply of pencils and erasers, clipboards and stopwatches and spare copies of the script. The stage manager will have discussed with the director if any cast members are absent and will have arranged for a suitable member of stage management or another member of the cast to read in for the absentee's part. Often actors are still working in a West End show or televising a series or sitcom when they are offered contracts for regional theatre, and their agent and the theatre management would agree a schedule to enable them to work around their prior commitment.

Once the layout of the rehearsal room and cover for the missing actors has been arranged, the director would ask everyone to sit down and he would discuss the play, the author, explore the meaning, characters, styles and accents. This discussion can sometimes run into several days should the play be deep and complex. The stage management should always attend these discussions, as they will have a better understanding of the play and why the director, designer and actors are very particular about some of the props. A read-through follows, the stage manager makes copious notes on props, fx and wardrobe

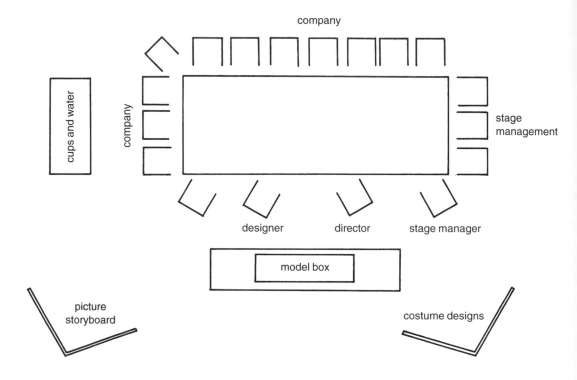

Setting up a room for a read-through using tables and screens.

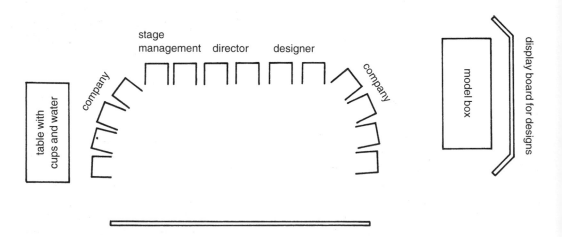

A rehearsal room set up for a read-through using a semicircle of chairs.

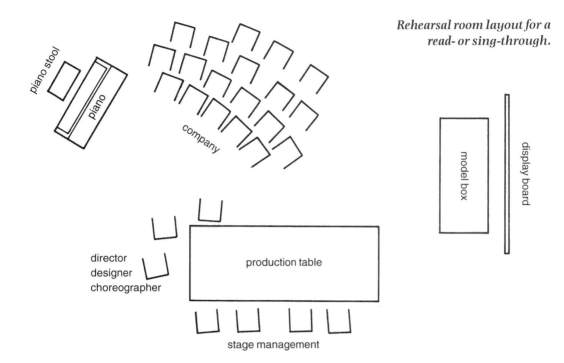

Rehearsal room layout for a read- or sing-through.

piano stool

piano

company

director
designer
choreographer

production table

stage management

model box

display board

settings. The DSM follows the script, timing the length of the scenes and acts, and noting any cuts in the text that the director has made. They will also make notes on any technical queries. The ASM may be busy reading in for a missing actor and making any necessary sound effect noises from baby cries to telephones ringing, as well as making cups of tea and coffee for the break.

The stage manager and ASM, even if they are reading in for one of the missing actors, will be listening to everything the director says about characterization and interpretation, making notes of relevant details. They will pay particular attention to notes on changes of script, set, costume or props. The team should meet later to discuss these notes, passing them onto the necessary heads of departments and as with all notes keeping a copy for themselves. The DSM will time the scenes and acts during the read-through. A director will often ask for

Producing Various Sound Fx in a Rehearsal Room

A small hand bell

A doorbell, battery and small push button mounted on a small piece of board. For rehearsals this bell can also stand in for telephone rings

Two pieces of batten 30cm long, to bang together, for the sound of gunshots and door bangs

A pea whistle, the type used on a sports field

Two pieces of sandpaper, rubbed together in different rhythms can sound like wind

A tubular bell, this makes a good substitute for a church bell or chiming clock

A rain stick, for water falling or indeed rain

A couple of old stage braces for various bangs and crashes

specific sequences to be timed, as this will help the director to know if the play needs to be cut not only for the overall length of the piece but for sections that may be too wordy or dull. The stage management have to pay careful attention to these cuts, as it's important to give full details of these to the electrics (Lx) department, sound (Snd) department and wardrobe (W/robe) department.

BLOCKING

It is important that your whole team keep accurate notes, including any cuts or changes to the script and have listened and keep listening intently to the director's discussions with the actors. These notes are also helpful for getting to know and understand the text well, recognizing the director's and designer's artistic interpretation of the play. But of all these notes the blocking is the most extensive as far as the DSM is concerned.

If the DSM is seated downstage below the marked setting line and level with the centre line, their view is then ideal for seeing the US (upstage) area which refers to the back of the stage furthest away from the audience; DS (downstage) area which refers to the nearest part of the stage to the audience; SR (stage right) and SL (stage left) are the areas right and left of the actors as they face DS towards the audience. To the DSM it is a mirror image when they block the actors as they are sitting at their table in an approximation of the front stalls, the actors left will be the audience right and the actors right will be the audience left.

Given this basic notation, a type of shorthand has evolved that helps the recording of blocking.

The diagrams opposite show the stage broken down into a major areas grid, and how to divide

The relative position of the stage management to the rest of the rehearsal room.

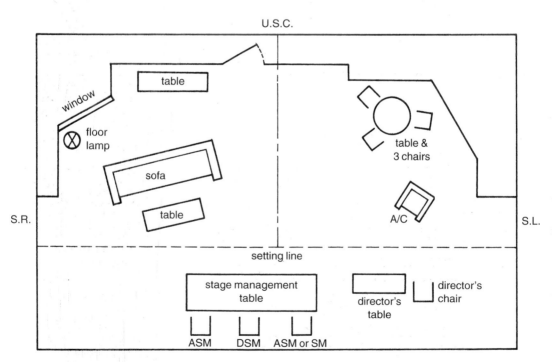

(Below) The stage divided up into the conventional areas and adapted according to the shape of the acting area.

(Below) Common blocking symbols.

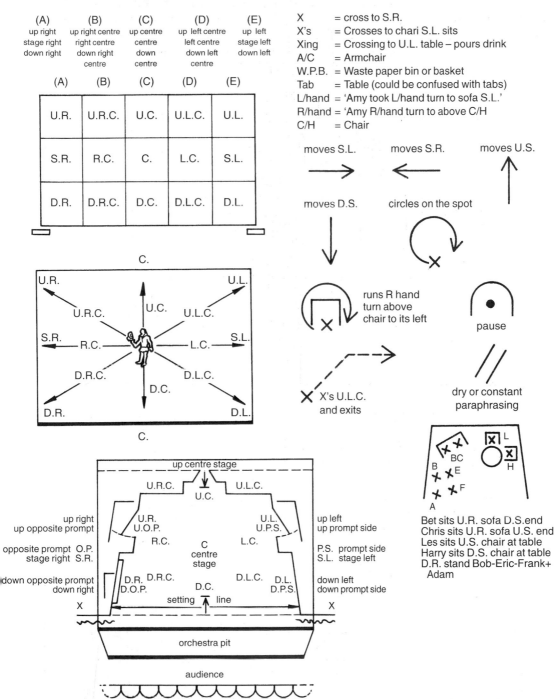

(A)	(B)	(C)	(D)	(E)
up right	up right centre	up centre	up left centre	up left
stage right	right centre	centre	left centre	stage left
down right	down right centre	down centre	down left centre	down left

(A)	(B)	(C)	(D)	(E)
U.R.	U.R.C.	U.C.	U.L.C.	U.L.
S.R.	R.C.	C.	L.C.	S.L.
D.R.	D.R.C.	D.C.	D.L.C.	D.L.

X = cross to S.R.
X's = Crosses to chari S.L. sits
Xing = Crossing to U.L. table – pours drink
A/C = Armchair
W.P.B. = Waste paper bin or basket
Tab = Table (could be confused with tabs)
L/hand = 'Amy took L/hand turn to sofa S.L.'
R/hand = 'Amy R/hand turn to above C/H
C/H = Chair

moves S.L.   moves S.R.   moves U.S.

moves D.S.   circles on the spot

runs R hand turn above chair to its left

pause

X X's U.L.C. and exits

dry or constant paraphrasing

Bet sits U.R. sofa D.S.end
Chris sits U.R. sofa U.S. end
Les sits U.S. chair at table
Harry sits D.S. chair at table
D.R. stand Bob-Eric-Frank+ Adam

C.

U.R.   U.L.
U.R.C.   U.C.   U.L.C.
S.R.   R.C.   L.C.   S.L.
D.R.C.   D.L.C.
D.C.
D.R.   D.L.

C.

up centre stage
U.R.C.   U.C.   U.L.C.

up right / up opposite prompt   U.R. U.O.P.   R.C.   C centre stage   L.C.   U.L. U.P.S.   up left / up prompt side

opposite prompt O.P. / stage right S.R.   P.S. prompt side / S.L. stage left

down opposite prompt / down right   D.R. D.O.P. D.R.C.   D.C.   D.L.C. D.L. D.P.S.   down left / down prompt side

X   setting ↑ line   X

orchestra pit

audience

53

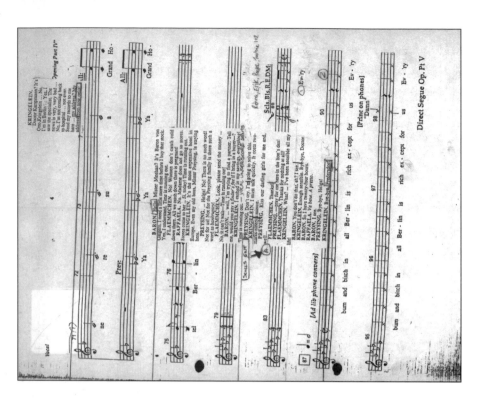

(Above) Marrying text and score for the prompt copy of a musical.

(Left) A page of text showing the correct way to document cuts in the text in order that they may be easily reinstated.

D. *John.* I remember.

Bora. I can, at any unseasonable instant of the night, appoint her to look out at her lady's chamber-window.

D. *John.* What life is in that, to be the death of this marriage?

Bora. The poison of that lies in you to temper. Go you to the Prince your brother; spare not to tell him that he hath wronged his honour in marrying the renowned Claudio—whose estimation do you mightily hold up—to a contaminated stale, such a one as Hero.

D. *John.* What proof shall I make of that?

Bora. Proof enough to misuse the Prince, to vex Claudio, to undo Hero, and kill Leonato. Look you for any other issue?

D. *John.* Only to despite them I will endeavour anything.

Bora. Go then, find me a meet hour to draw Don Pedro and the Count Claudio alone: tell them that you know that Hero loves me; intend a kind of zeal both to the Prince and Claudio—as in love of your brother's honour, who hath made this match, and his friend's reputation, who is thus like to be cozened with the semblance of a maid—that you have discovered thus. They will scarcely believe this without trial offer them such instances, which shall bear no less likelihood than to see me at her chamber-window, hear me call Margaret Hero,

21. *temper*] mix, compound.
24. *estimation*] worth, or repute: both senses are implied.
25. *contaminated stale*] polluted wanton. *OED* quotes this to illustrate one of the meanings derived from *stale* (= decoy bird).
28. *misuse...vex*] delude....distress

33. Don] Q (don); on F.   36. in] Q; in a F.

Shakespeare's only use of the word as a verb; cf. Anon, *The Rare Triumphs of Love and Fortune* (Hazlitt's *Dodsley*, vi.150)—'What lives or draweth breath, but I can pleasure or *despite*?'
35. *intend*] profess, pretend, as in *R3*, III.vii.45—'*intend* some fear'.
39. *cozened*] cheated.

the different acting areas that various theatres present; in the round there is a north, south, east or west approach or divide the acting area into four, calling each area 1, 2, 3, and 4 or ABC&D, each entrance would be a letter or number or the name of certain characters – for example 'Ken's entrance' or 'Emma's entrance'. Whatever the situation, the important thing is that the system is clear and consistent and is known to all the staging departments and designers. This is particularly relevant when touring, so it is worthwhile making sure your symbols translate to any theatre. There are many other symbols and hieroglyphics that may be used.

A reminder of the layout of the prompt copy: the page of text is on the right-hand side as you look at the script and a blank sheet of paper on the left-hand side; you then divide the blank sheet into two columns with a pencilled line; the blocking will now be entered in the column furthest away from the text. The numbering of each move starts with a bracketed number within the text. It is important that these numbers accurately reflect the actor's moves. They must always relate to a specific word, syllable, space between words or immediately after a sentence, but never just in the margin. Often an actor will not remember a certain line because they have forgotten their move – the two things go together. There may only be one or two moves on each page of text or there may be twenty-eight or thirty; sometimes one move can take up to half a page of writing depending on the action. The numbers of each move within the text must line up with the same number and notation in the blocking column, this numbering is consecutive and starts again at one with each new page otherwise you would end up with several thousand moves by the end of a script. It is also much easier to amend if a page of script is cut or changed.

It is helpful to make small stage diagrams marking the actors' positions with small cross-

es and their character initial by the side of each cross; this system is an especially good one when the cast is large with maybe up to twenty people on stage all moving at approximately the same time.

As the rehearsal progresses and actors and director get more involved and imaginations start to flow, the DSM will add extra notes into the blocking such as when an actor or actress picks up a glass of drink or opens a book or blows their nose or drops a stitch while knitting and so on, these details are important to an actor's timing or another actor's entrance or perhaps to a relevant Snd or Lx cue during the action.

The changes to the blocking often come quickly and constantly and the DSM must be careful and accurate in recording this and deal with all changes as they happen. As discussions occur between a director and actor and the change is rehearsed it is advisable to bracket cuts in the text rather than delete completely. If a whole page is taken out put this page at the back of your folder, as there is a possibility it may be reinstated later. If a page is full of brackets and lines then retype the text as it will be too confusing when you come to put the cues into the script. It is advisable to keep copies of all the cut pages and changed text in the production file, and date each one as it occurs.

It very important to tidy up a script and alter any blocking at the time. Never leave any of it until the next day or later as there will be no time to catch up and you will have forgotten the necessary details.

The music pause, an upside down U with a dot in the middle, is used for a pause within the text. The symbol // is usually used for marking an actor's troublesome lines where they dry (forget their lines) or paraphrase (get the sense but not all the words that are written!). Mark your script with these two lines beside the speech or piece of text that the actor is finding

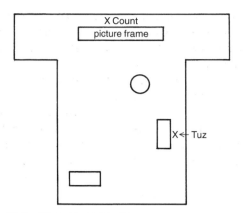

(1) Tuz X's behind table S.L.
Count ents through picture frame
V X's to Tuz

(2) ANF brings letter to V
V opens letter

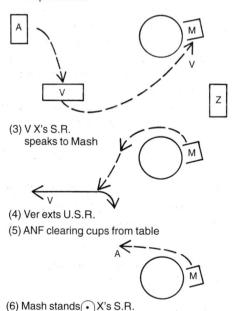

(3) V X's S.R.
speaks to Mash

(4) Ver exts U.S.R.
(5) ANF clearing cups from table

(6) Mash stands(•)X's S.R.

An example of blocking using small diagrams as well as symbols.

difficult. Make a note of the speech, character's name and page number, tell the actor in a break or at the end of rehearsals – sometimes the actors will ask you for a copy of these notes. This is where all the early preparation is so important for stage management, particularly the DSM who needs to listen to all discussions between the director and actors. They will then know why it is important that lines are not missed or paraphrased, that the wrong emphasis, or punctuation can totally alter a storyline.

PROMPTING

During a rehearsal the DSM needs to realize when to give that much-needed word or line that the actor knew so well the night before but that now totally eludes him. During performance, text may vanish from the mind because a member of the audience talks very loudly during the play or they fan themselves with their programme during a dramatic pause; perhaps the actor is tired having rehearsed another play during the day, and driven several miles from the rehearsal room to the theatre or the FOH manager has allowed late-comers into the auditorium.

To be able to prompt well a DSM must learn a few techniques. First of all they must be sensitive to the feelings and moods of the cast, understand the characters that the actors are playing and the play. They need to be aware of how an actor likes to be prompted by asking them whether they require a full sentence, one word or an operative word. Some actors are taught and encouraged to stop and call 'line' which many experienced actors and directors find breaks the mood and concentration. Part of the DSM technique is to sense when an actor has dried (forgotten their lines) by the way they stand or walk across the stage or, ad-lib (make up a passage of text on the spur of the moment to fit in with the scene) or look frantically over to the stage management table in the rehearsal room or the prompt corner when in performance with an appealing terrified look.

You must have the confidence to take your eyes off the book to look at the actors as you follow the text; it is possible to do this if you roll your pencil down the page making sure you are one line ahead of the actor. This helps you to memorize the line briefly to enable you to lift your eyes and look at the troubled actor who may not be in trouble but has decided to put in a pause. Another way is to mouth the words as they are spoken so if they stop you are right there with them. Never whisper a prompt or mumble, whether in rehearsal or performance, especially performance, as there is nothing worse than an unfortunate actor not being able to hear the prompt and having it repeated several times before they are able to pick up the scene; the line spoken loudly and with confidence will be heard by the audience and forgotten, the other way it is noticed and not forgotten, and makes the actor look bad and under-rehearsed. Never prompt with just the single word 'the' or 'of' as this would not help anyone to remember the whole sentence, the company may need to know who has dried and the DSM may have to say the character's name, for example, Mary ... 'your briefcase is on the table'. Sometimes the actor dries because they have forgotten a piece of action such as crossing the stage or sitting on a sofa and this action will actually give them the forgotten line, so it's quite in order for the DSM to prompt their action, for example a character may have the line ... 'I will wait here for Robert' ... and the move that is ... *Mary X's to sofa U.L. & sits*. The DSM would give the prompt *cross to sofa & sit*; the actress would then remember to say the line as she crosses to sit on the sofa. Occasionally this may happen in performance, especially if the play is very active.

The cast need to be able to trust the DSM; this is why they must always be the one in rehearsal

every day, to enable the actors to become familiar with their voice. This does not mean that if necessary the ASM cannot stand in for them. However, because rehearsals are a practice for performance, the DSM must familiarize themselves with the individual actor, the characters and the play. This will help you to learn the pace of the play, which is vital if you are to cue the lights, sound and other effects sensitively during the technical rehearsal and performances.

CALL SHEETS

From the day of the first read-through a call sheet will be required. Call sheets should be laid out in a specific format. They must be clear, informative and accurate. This should include the names of the directors in attendance, as there may be several calls at the same time in different venues with different personnel taking these rehearsals. All these many pieces of documentation are a necessary tool for the stage management team and become the main links to the production as a whole, helping communication between company, creative team, staging departments and administration.

CCs is a list of all the personnel who require a copy of the document. This is also a checklist

---

Different Types of Call Sheets

Call sheets are a specifically laid-out document for any call required. They would come under the following titles:

Rehearsal calls	Band calls
Dance calls	Music calls
Movement calls	Song or singing
Fight calls	calls
Voice calls	Chorus calls
Wardrobe calls	Publicity and or
Wig calls	Press calls

'ACCRINGTON PALS'

Venue: The Drill Hall St John Street   **Date:** Monday January 9th 1999

Telephone: xxxx xxxx

CALL:

10.30am	Act 1 Sc 3	Miss Ellie Mills
		Miss Jo Roberts
11.30am	Act 1 Sc 4	Mr Robert Brown (to join)
11.45am	COFFEE BREAK	
12.00 noon	Continue as above	
1.00pm	LUNCH BREAK	
2.15pm	Run of Act 1	Full company
4.00pm	TEA BREAK	
4.15pm	Notes and work sections	Full company
5.30pm	Call ends	

Signed:

Stage Manager

cc: Director/designer/Lx/Snd/Dsm/W/robe/movement/voice/etc.

A call sheet.

of who has been informed. They would be listed by surname in alphabetical order.

The stage manager has to make sure the call sheets are accurate, up to date, and very clear to the reader. Without these vital pieces of paper the rehearsal process would grind to a halt. The stage manager in conjunction with the director has to make sure it fits in with the plans of the various members of the staging departments and creative teams. Sometimes these schedules have to be so tightly organized it only needs someone to be ill or not turn up

Company, Creative Teams, Staging Departments and Administration

Company	Staging
All the actors	Departments
	Workshop
Creative Teams	Paintshop
Director	Props
Set Designer	Department
Costume Designer	Lx Department
Lighting Designer	Sound
Sound Designer	Department
Choreographer	Wardrobe
Musical Director	
Conductor	Administration
Movement, Voice	Chief Executive
and Fight	Production
specialists	Secretary
	Publicity
	Marketing
	Box Office
	FOH Manager

and the whole day is thrown into chaos, time wasted and monies lost.

The following is a good example of how this happened on a large star-studded musical and was not the careless fault of a heavily burdened stage manager. In the Midlands on one cold, wet Monday in the penultimate week of the rehearsal period all the calls had been planned in finite detail, all the company and relevant creative team had been given the information and paperwork to back it up plus call sheets on the notice-boards. The calls consisted of:

Text calls for three of the principals rehearsing on stage at the theatre where the show would be opening. 10:00am–1:00pm.

Dance calls with twenty chorus in a drill hall two miles across the city. 11:00am–1:00pm.

Music calls with the musical director (MD) in a local church hall a 15-min walk from the theatre for all six principals plus three of the dancers who sang with one of the principals; these calls were 45min apart. 10:00am–1:30pm.

Wardrobe calls for fittings with the main male and female lead 50min each 10:00am and 10:50am (ending at 11:30am).

Wig fittings for the above two from 11:30am–1:00pm. The designer for wigs and hats was travelling from Wales to the Midlands having had a previous appointment. They were on a tricky travel timetable, but would be on time.

Wardrobe flagged up an extra call last thing the night before for shoe fittings for the chorus all day at 10-min intervals stating that they would travel to the rehearsal room if necessary.

The stage manager received a phone call at 8:30am from the leading man to say that he would not be in attendance that day as he was rehearsing for a TV sitcom. After an exclamation of surprise from the SM, the actor then replied 'Oh! did I not mention this TV rehearsal? I'm sure I told someone', but of course he could not remember to whom he had mentioned it. The knock-on effect of this piece of news was huge. The stage manager began to stop the impending chaos by phoning various members of the creative team and had to think very fast on his feet as to how the schedule could be rearranged. But the day had started, the hat and wig designer was already travelling to the first appointment and would have no access to a telephone (the mobile phone did not seem to be working) before reaching the Midlands. The choreographer had already planned to the minute their separate dance call with the missing leading man before catching their train to a TV studio in York two days previously. The MD had planned with the sound department a session and a studio to record some of the click track.

After a lot of phone calls, meetings and rearranging of this chaotic day, it turned out reasonably well, but not before several plans had to be cut and put forward into the already tight schedule of the final week of rehearsals. It also meant that various members of the creative team had to be paid for hours that they had already been committed to but in fact did not work because of the revised schedule. An expensive experience for the theatre management.

FITTINGS

The stage manager must work closely with the wardrobe department and the costume designer. The first contact is when the stage manager sends out scripts and a welcome letter to each member of the cast. The actors will receive and fill in an enclosed blank measurement form and bring it with them on the day of the read-through. The stage management will collect these forms and hand them to the wardrobe supervisor. Those actors who have not filled in the form will be measured there and then in the rehearsal room before the read-through or any production discussions begin.

The wardrobe department will inform the stage manager of any call required in the near future – whom they need and for what character (the actor could be doubling parts), the day, time and place of the fitting, as it could take place at a hire company, the wardrobe department at the theatre or at rehearsals in an adjoining room. The stage manager often has to assist the wardrobe supervisor as to where the fittings will take place by organizing the best venue to suit the rehearsal calls. If the actor is rehearsing a scene whereby they are never off the stage, the rehearsal room is the best place, as the director will not have to put an extra half an hour onto the call for travel time and the actor ends up being less stressed. If it is a hire firm in the next city to the theatre or London involving a couple of hours' travel time, the

---

Click Track

This is the recorded sound of the chorus singing their songs that is then played while they dance. The audience rather than hearing out-of-breath dancers see fast, complicated choreography while the company are apparently singing their hearts out.

---

arrangement has to be discussed with the director as it could be a half or whole day away from the rehearsal room. The costume designer must attend all fittings and wardrobe calls, so their availability and travel has to be considered, plus those of the other members of the creative team such as wig and hat designers. The stage manager and/or the director will often attend fittings especially if there is to be a complex costume with a character who has a lot of physical action as part of their role, or stage blood is going to used, or a microphone pack worn, special pockets required and so on. The call sheets are laid out in exactly the same way as the rehearsal sheets, stating the venue and which of the creative team will be in attendance.

There may be a request from the designer and the wardrobe for the actor to bring along various pieces of underwear to help the costume fit. As the fittings progress they will often take longer, sometimes up to an hour as accessories are added, that is, shoes, jewellery, scarves, wigs and hats. Actresses are sometimes asked if they can use their own hair or just a hairpiece, actors a toupee or grow their own moustache and beard. Should this not be the case then a piece of the artiste's own hair is sent to a wig firm and with some input from the designer the toupee, moustache, beard, or hairpiece is made up to the required colour. The stage management need to make sure all this happens and is followed through.

SPECIALIST ADVISERS

Often a stage manager will be called upon to look for someone with a knowledge of special subjects, such as a doctor or someone from the army, because there are many shows that require scenes to be performed authentically by the actors in subject areas they know nothing about. There is nothing worse than an actor holding a firearm incorrectly or someone dying of a heart attack or giving birth to a baby in the wrong way, causing the audience to laugh during a very serious sensitive moment within the show.

A good example is the play *The Long and the Short and the Tall* by Willis Hall that is set in the Malayan jungle in 1942 during the Second World War. The company of soldiers in the story look upon their duty with little enthusiasm, but before the end of the play they have faced up to many unforeseen dangers. Within the acts and scenes the actors have to really understand what it is like to fight side by side, and kill, plus the knowledge of possibly being killed by the enemy, use weapons, clean them, drill, think, walk and talk like soldiers. So help from a military adviser for this production would be essential.

There are often experts called in to help with the correct way of speaking a foreign language. There was once an actor playing the part of a Chinese servant. The part was small and the actor only had three lines to say in the oriental language. He thought that he would be able to cope with this by asking the help of the local Chinese restaurant. After a week of struggling with the words and trying to remember the various inflections that were required, as the same words said with different emphasis could mean vastly different things, he had these three lines mastered, or so he thought, until the first night when the waiters of the restaurant had taken up the offer of complimentary seats for the play. When the actor came to his scene he spoke his lines loudly and clearly. There was total silence from the audience except the three waiters who

were rolling in the aisles with mirth as the actor had delivered the small speech with the correct words but the wrong inflection. He had asked the leading lady to kiss the rotting fish in the kitchen instead of telling her a light supper would be prepared for her and left in the kitchen. The actor did master these three lines after more visits to the restaurant and he managed to keep the inflections under control until the end of the play's run. However, it is important for stage management to look for those specialist requirements within a show. There is always advice of some kind needed in most productions.

STAND-IN PROPS AND FURNITURE

Props and furniture for the early rehearsals are always substitute items, as it takes time to acquire the real things. If you need to hire anything then the budget will only allow these items to be hired for the shortest possible period; usually from the day before the technical rehearsal. As rehearsals progress and various action and stage business is tried there is no knowing whether the designed or apparently

Items from your prop cupboard labelled to become stand-in props.

61

obvious items will work, then decisions are made and the DSM will send rehearsal notes out to the SM team before props or furniture are bought or hired. The most important job for the stage management is to make sure the substitutes are close to the real thing in size, shape and weight, whether it is a cigarette lighter or a trunk, which also applies to the furniture. It is no use a sofa being able to seat two people have a high back and thin wooden arms or be two upright chairs tied together when it needs to be something that will accommodate at least three people sitting, as an actor has to lie full length on it or sit on the arms or back. It is necessary for the DSM to help the stage manager and team by making sure they pass on detailed information as to what happens to the furniture in the play's action, whether anyone does lie on the sofa, sit on the arms or jump, sit or lean over the back, jump up onto the seat, throw food or liquid over the upholstery. In one show a beautiful, delicate period wicker sofa was hired for a scene in a conservatory when the whole company were on stage having afternoon tea, the leading man had been blocked to jump up onto the delicate piece and fell straight through – he was all of fourteen stone and furniture is not made for that kind of treatment unless it has been specially designed to accommodate that action. The DSM had never mentioned this action assuming it would be a robust sofa, and never checked or thought it through. Never assume, as the saying goes – assumption is the mother of all foul-ups!

If chairs are being used for cupboards or shelves you must label what each item is standing in for, as both actor and director can misinterpret the various pieces of furniture and expect to be able to use them in a way contrary to their design.

The other items to label and follow through in their use are the smaller props, especially crockery such as plates and bowls. It is not practical to use real food in rehearsal, as you need the facili-

Chairs in the rehearsal room used as a stand-in bookshelf.

ties to prepare or cook it. It is not popular to ask an actor to eat food over and over again while the scene is being perfected. All the correct foodstuffs are usually used in the final run-through before the technical rehearsal. In the play *How the Other Half Lives* by Alan Ayckbourn there is a complex plot involving two dinner parties happening on two supposedly different evenings in two different houses. The scene starts with the preparation for the dinner, laying the table, waiting for the guests to arrive, and the meal itself. In one production the setting was a specially built table in the style of a plus sign with a two-coloured table cloth and four swivel dining chairs. Both houses had a three-course meal, one cordon bleu on expensive china and good wine out of expensive glasses; the second house was serving soup and hot rolls followed by pasta on cheap china plates with cheap plonk and beer out of cans. For this production the stage management had to have specific rehearsals with all the food because of the very difficult timing of eating and talking. There were then three run-throughs with a full menu. By the time they had worked a technical rehearsal, two dress rehearsals and eight performances each week for four weeks, the cast between shows and at all meal breaks began to follow very spartan diets.

Substitute costumes are allowed in rehearsal if the wardrobe department can find suitable items. It is highly unlikely to be the real clothes because, if they are being made by the theatre's own staff nothing would be ready to wear at the time of the early rehearsals. If anything is hired it would be far too expensive to acquire for the rehearsal period plus performances, also after several weeks in a dusty church hall everything would be dishevelled and unfit to wear. Rehearsal costumes need to be in keeping with the period of the play. If it were set in the Victorian times all the actresses would be given practice skirts and possibly corsets plus heeled shoes or button boots by the wardrobe department. Because of today's mode of dress and our way of moving and sitting the assistance of these pieces of clothing is very important to the performer. The men would need high wing collars and tight jackets plus any padding for paunches, the same for actresses if any of them are meant to be pregnant.

STORAGE SPACE IN A REHEARSAL ROOM

It is advisable to lay out a rehearsal room as near to the space and shape of the stage and wing area as possible. This gives the company and director as well as the stage management team an idea of how the show will work in the venue's performing space. It can be difficult when the hall is often a lot smaller than the acting area, with a mark-out of the set on the floor, to store carefully all the items that may be needed – for example, tables for the stage management and director, the prop tables and props, any furniture for other acts and scenes within the play as well as chairs for the actors to sit on

and somewhere to put their bags and outdoor clothes. It needs some careful consideration. There might be a rope or object suspended from the ceiling of the hall, something that will later be flown in the theatre or a steel deck with some small set pieces added to assist the actors in understanding the mechanics of a sequence. Stepladders are another much used prop along with electric cable trailing across the room from the stage management table to the working electrical item on stage. With all this clutter Health and Safety issues are an important consideration as it is essential that the company are not injured in any way; the best people to monitor this are the stage management team.

HEALTH AND SAFETY

A stage manager once arrived back at the church hall after a lunch break to find some of the company who had arrived early for the afternoon call rehearsing their scenes on the top of a rather shaky trestle table, with an old wooden stepladder and on a highly polished floor. The potential dangers of this scenario gave the stage manager a tremendous fright. The Health and Safety rules do not just apply to performances. There have to be discussions before a show starts rehearsing to make sure all potential dangers are covered. It is so easy for stage management to think that because they are working in a public building and hired premises all aspects of Health and Safety regulations are observed, but that is not necessarily the case. A stage manager also never knows when a member of the company or a director will get carried away with inventive ideas forgetting all aspects of safety. Always check thoroughly before a show goes into rehearsal and certainly before it transfers to a theatre. If a play requires a firearm to fire it is advisable to contact an accredited theatrical supplier such as Bapty and Co. Ltd, Middlesex, as well as New Scotland Yard firearms department. Dummies may be used with sound effects, but many directors do

RISK ASSESSMENT

| Title (*Task/premises*) | Rehearsal and performance period of 'How to Succeed in Business' | | | | | | | | | |

| Location/Dept | Guildhall School of Music & Drama, rooms 147, 250, 251, 252, LTB | Ref. No | | Assessor Name(s) | | | Lone Schacksen | | | |

Activity / Plant / Materials	Hazard	Persons at Risk (No/Type)	Comments, existing controls, references used	*Risk Evaluation			Proposed Controls or Action & References Required	Revised Risk Evaluation (after control measures in place or action has been taken)		
				Severity	Likelihood	Rating		Severity	Likelihood	Rating
Choreographed activities involving standing on and / or dancing on tables and chairs	Slips, falls and trips	up to 12 acting students	Tables and chairs are not specifically designed for this purpose.	Moderate	Unlikely	High	**Work (rehearsals involving the tables & chairs) must not be started until the risk has been reduced.** A new table must be found for these scenes. New table found. Chairs must be mended where applicable. Chairs mended.	Moderate	Highly unlikely	Low
Using flats for the performance	Unstable flats	12 acting students Director/MD Choreographer Stage Management	The flats provided by the drama department are extremely unstable, and subject to falling over.	High	Likely	High	Stage weights must be used to stabilize the flats and prevent them from falling over. Stage weights found.	High	Unlikely	Medium
Rehearsals in GSMD Rehearsal Rooms	Heat	12 acting students Director/MD Choreographer Stage Management	Rooms have little or no ventilation facilities. Fans have been provided to circulate air, but room temperature remains extremely high during rehearsals, especially when dance-orientated.	Slight	Unlikely	Low	Matter referred to Physical Services for review. Project in place to install air handling/air conditioning systems throughout building. Air circulation system installed in 147 for performances.	N/A	N/A	N/A

| * Refer to the Corporation Code of Practice on Risk Assessment. | Signature(s): | | Date Completed: | 24 May 2000 2.00pm |

not like this as much as hearing the live sound. However, whatever decision is made there are several rules of safety to be taken into account.

Weapons must never be left unattended on a prop table. It is advisable to have someone specifically in charge of the guns so that one can be loaded just before handing to the actor and received from them as they exit from the stage. The weapons must be thoroughly checked and empty of blanks before and after use, always kept in a locked cupboard, with the key kept only by the person specifically in charge of the weapons. Never allow actors to fool around with guns by pointing them at each other or generally waving them about unless it is a specifically blocked piece of action on stage. Always have a gun practice away from the rehearsal room and before the technical rehearsals on stage with relevant warning notices posted on notice-boards around the theatre and rehearsal room, and sufficient verbal warning before any firing.

Safety precautions also have to be taken for swords, daggers and knives of any kind. Always make sure the company has a professional fight instructor to teach them all how to handle these weapons, from a knife to a fencing or flat-bladed sword. The awkward ones to handle are the heavy, long two-handed double-edged swords used in period battle scenes, especially on a small-ish stage where there must be reasonable space between actors and set. There should always be a fight call before a show every day, and be very strict with actors who decide to change the action with weapons during a performance; they must be severely dealt with as this is a very dangerous action for an actor to take. If the fight director has changed moves after seeing that they did not work very well on the first night, then the stage manager must be informed. Swords as well as guns must be checked for wear and tear after each performance.

If hot water is to be used for washing or drinking then it must never be boiling. Treat slippery surfaces and make sure, if possible, that shoes have rubber soles, take care when the cast are running up and down treads and rakes, ensure that off-stage treads have handrails, help actors off-stage with the aid of a torch when they have to run from bright stage lighting to darkness and blue working light behind the set. All areas are potential hazards unless suitably addressed:

OPPOSITE PAGE
A completed risk assessment sheet.

Fight sequence for a Shakespeare play. Note the potentially dangerous flooring as well as the swords.

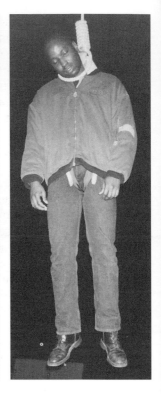

A rehearsal for a hanging. Stage management try out the noose (above left) before the actors are introduced to the rig. It is important to make sure the rope noose is fixed securely and the noose then attached to a harness worn under the costume. The result gives the impression of the actor hanging by his neck, but the rope is not in fact touching the neck. (Above, middle) The actor's turn to try out the hanging sequence. (Above, right) The actor tests the rig.

Another potential hazard: a get-off ladder.

stage weights, braces and battens should be painted white or covered in white gaffer tape. A lot of these points can be thought about when setting up rehearsal rooms and watching run-throughs of scenes or the whole show, and worries taken to the production manager to enable prior warning and prevention of accidents.

RUNNING SCRIPTS

Every member of stage management should have a running copy. This script starts being worked on from day one of rehearsals, the layout of the scripts are the same as a prompt copy without the moves. The stage manager's version should have as many cues marked down as possible having taken some of them from the DSM who would have gleaned quite a lot from the rehearsal period. The director may indicate a change of location or light, the sound of birds, cars arriving and departing or thumps and bangs, or the text specifies a change. They would also have noted from where actors come on and whether they will be able to see and hear or would need a cue light for their entrance.

Props will be collected from the actors at certain times or a door needs to be held open for them, a tray to be handed to them or their costume adjusted, a hat put on or an apron tied as the dressers are probably busy elsewhere. There may be live cues such as crashes, bangs or whistles, a pot of tea to be made for a meal scene, the clingfilm or cooking foil taken off the sandwiches before they go on stage. In one of the famous séance scenes in the play *Blithe Spirit* by Noel Coward the stage management in their haste with the scene changes had forgotten to take the clingfilm off the sandwiches and because the film was pulled taut you could not see it when the lights went up. Soon the line came, 'Do have a sandwich Madame Arcati', 'Oh', she replied 'how delicious, may I have two?' There was silence then some very obvious giggles from the cast on-stage. The scene

nonetheless carried on to its end. When they all came off-stage they were in fits of laughter as the actress playing Madame Arcati thought she had lost the feeling in her fingers as she struggled to pick up the sandwiches and had taken the whole plate when she went off-stage! Always mark jobs of that nature in heavy pencil or highlighter; it is so easy to forget about them. This is why a running script is so important, because running a show can change from performance to performance. With timings on scenes altering and items getting lost or broken, this can distract a member of stage management and small tasks are completely forgotten. A running script is also a useful prompt to confirm where you are in the show.

RUNNING LISTS

Running lists are the pieces of paper that state the order of the jobs each member of stage management does throughout the performance, with timings as to when the task happens and with whom they may do the scene change or open shutters or doors, as well as which side of the stage the task takes place. A copy of this list is pinned to the wall in the wings and on the clipboards belonging to individual members of stage management. These lists are for quick reference especially if you have rushed off-stage right and have to re-enter in a few seconds on-stage left perhaps with a chair to set on specific marks. If you suddenly forget what you have to do next it is important that there are these lists to quickly refer to.

SETTING LISTS

Setting lists document all props furniture and dressing positions both on-stage and off right and left, these lists are used to set up the show from the top of Act 1 to the end of the play. These lists, as with other documents, start from the first rehearsal and adjust and evolve as the weeks

'THE SNOWMAIDEN'

STAGE RIGHT RUNNING LIST – LAURA STREATHER ASM

Pre-show

Time	Action	Operator
–50 mins	Shout check	Megan Phillips Sarah Morgan
–50 mins	Fill bowls in studio dressing rooms with water	Laura Streather
–20mins	Fill and turn tea urn on	Laura Streather
–15mins	Collect valuables from studio dressing rooms	Laura Streather
–5mins	Make tea in teapot – 8 teabags	Laura Streather
Beginners	Put battery in clock on stage	Laura Streather

Prologue

Beginners	Mr Adrian Dwyer	on stage
	Miss Joana Cunha	SR wing
	Miss Cinzia Barbotti	SR behind flat
	Miss Isabel Clegg	SR behind flat
	Miss Karen Mok	SR behind flat
	Miss Maria Nikoloulea	SR behind flat
	Mr Luke Baio	SR behind flat

Page	Area	Action	Operator
1	USR	Turn air pressure on	Laura Streather – clearance from Sarah
3	CSR	Page door shut after Adrian's exit	Laura Streather
3	USR	Page door shut after Spring's exit	Laura Streather
3	DSR	Page door open for Spring's entr. Close once lights have faded	Laura Streather
	Off SR	Assist maid with trolley & wait off SR	Laura Streather
8	DSR	Maid enters with trolley. Page door open and close once entered	Laura Streather
10	DSR	Maid exits with coat. Page door open and close once exited	Laura Streather Kate John **Q light given**

13	DSR	Dancers enter as birds. Page door open and close once ent.	Laura Streather **Q light given**
16–18	Off SR	Collect watering can and trowel and wait by DSR door	Laura Streather
19	DSR	Dancers exit DSR. Page door open and leave open – maid exits with trolley	Laura Streather
19	SR	SR flipper flat closes. Open CSR door	Louise Rogers
20	Off SR	Return trolley to pre-set	Laura Streather Kate John
	Off SR	Check mic is on for off-stage chorus	Laura Streather Sarah Morgan
35	SR	Flipper flat opens with Father Frost in chair. Leave DSR door open until he starts singing	Laura Streather
37	CSR	Wood Spirit enters CSR with silver salver	Laura Streather
43	CSR	Open door for maids entr. With suitcase. Close once entered	Laura Streather
48		SR flat moves to perpendicular position	Adrian Dwyer
50		Collect male chorus from dressing room	Laura Streather
67	USR	Snowmaiden exits. Page door open and leave for carnival scene	Louise Rogers

A running list showing that the first action is required well before the start of the performance.

proceed until everyone meets on-stage for the technical rehearsal. During the technical it is decided if the setting lists work, if not they will be changed. Because there is not time during the running of the show to delve into prop rooms or cupboards the show is set up in its entirety each day. Depending on the size of the production this can take up to two hours before the doors open to the public. The rundown to the opening of those doors starts with the stage being swept, mopped or vacuumed, and the furniture dusted, polished and set on coloured marks; each of these marks may have had specific lights focused onto them and there is usually a different colour for each scene that should be noted on the setting lists. Any furniture brought on for other scenes is set on the relevant sides of the stage. This is listed on the off-stage setting lists and within the written lists there are diagrams of how each prop is set. This is very necessary as actors, once the show has been blocked, will expect and need each prop to be in the same place every time the show is rehearsed or performed, as it affects their timing. An actor running from stage left to right needed to pick up a newspaper folded in a certain way from the prop table as he was running. The paper had been set

OFF-STAGE RIGHT:

On props table:

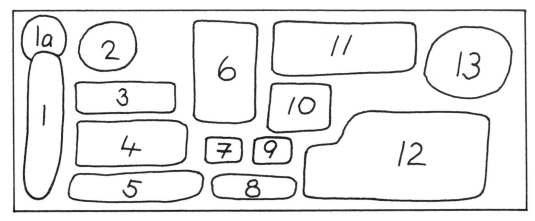

(1) wild fake flowers   1 red carnation
                         1 white lily
                         1 blue forget-me-not
                         1 spare white feather flower
                         for dome
(1a) pot of talc for dome flower
(2) coloured flower head garland
(3) 14 pairs of sun spectacles
     (matching metal frames)
(4) wooden-handled trowel

(5) fake rose for the Heron
(6) 14 white cane sticks
     (1in diameter and 18in long)
(7) 1 white handkerchief (man's)
(8) scroll
(9) gold-leafed ring box (in it) pearl
(10) 14 white handkerchiefs (men's)
(11) Whisky tumblers
(12) Flower trug with 14 red roses
(13) Bowl of snowflakes

Setting list from **The Snowmaiden** *showing details of a props table.*

at the back of the prop table and not folded in its usual way. He hesitated and missed an important entrance which another actor had to react to; there was also a sound cue to her reaction that, as a consequence, did not happen and rather spoilt the scene. All because the stage management did not think it mattered to have the props set in exactly the same place every performance. To ensure this level of accuracy there needs to be several comprehensive setting lists.

Sometimes setting lists show that some of the settings are extremely detailed, for example the spout of the teapot is facing upstage as you look at it with the handle towards the actor as they pick up the tray, all the handles of the cups are facing to the right of the handler, only one has

a teaspoon (the only character in the scene that needs to use a spoon), the remaining cups do not as it would impede the timing of the action required. The tablecloth is folded in a specific way to help the actor lay the table quickly while speaking. The top on the whisky bottle is loosened for quick, safe handling. The box of matches has two matches protruding from the matchbox so that the actor does not pick up the box upside down – the matches would then fall from the box and the timed action ruined. The string on the parcel is tied in a loose slipknot to help with easy opening, letter envelopes are sealed just by the tip of the flap preventing a longwinded ugly moment as the actor tries in vain to open a well-stuck envelope.

Setting list from **The Reluctant Debutante** *showing the whole stage.*

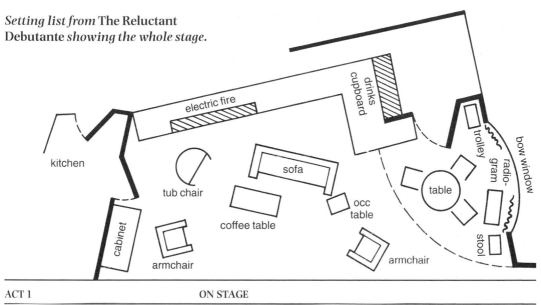

ACT 1			ON STAGE
D.R.	CABINET	ON TOP	(1) Lamp (switched off) (2) Vase of flowers (Roses) (3) Ashtray (empty) (4) Small ornament (Statue)
	IN CABINET	TOP SHELF MID SHELF BOT SHELF	China Tea Set 3 Vases/2 Paper weights 2 China Dogs
R.C	ARMCHAIR	IN IT	Cushion
U.R.	MANTLESHELF	ON IT	Invitation Cards (10) Notebook and Pencil Open Cigarette Box (½ full) Table Lighter Bottle of Specs Cleaning Fluid Soft Cloth
U.L.C.	DRINKS CUPBOARD	ON IT	Tray of drinks … Bottle Vermouth Bottle of Gin Decanters: Whisky Brandy Port Various Glasses Soda Syphon Jug of Water Mixers Large Ashtray Pair of earrings behind ashtray
L.C.	ON TABLE		Breakfast items as drawing 3 cups & saucers & spoons 3 Large plates of Poached Egg 3 Small Plates Butter dish & Butter & knife Milk Jug (½ full) Coffee Pot Hot water Jug Sugar Bowl (½ full) & spoon

71

This detailed information comes from experience handed down over the generations of stage management and also by requests from the actors to the DSM and ASM during the rehearsal process, along with final details from the technical rehearsal. Because of the constant changes likely to occur through the progress of a production it is advisable to handwrite all working documents until the very last moment, often as late as the opening night and a few days beyond, certainly until you feel the show has settled.

High standards of efficiency come from good communication. Every day you must update all working papers plus illustrations, graphs and diagrams. Discuss these changes with your team in great detail so everyone has correct and accurate information.

PROGRESS MEETINGS

Progress meetings are another important aspect of collating a show. These meetings are essential. All the queries and decisions made affect more than one of the staging departments and the only way to make sure everyone is up to the same understanding and awareness of the progress of the show is to meet on a regular basis. Usually the meetings take place every two weeks throughout a six-week rehearsal period, however this can vary depending on the demands of the production. The production manager will chair these meetings, the stage manager will have liaised closely with the PM and both will have made an agenda. This would be a list of concerns that may have arisen during the rehearsal or while the set was evolving in the workshop or just the simple questions of how the work is coming along? Is everyone up to schedule? The rehearsal reports of various notes from past rehearsals would be read through with necessary attention given to the problems and queries of each department. The type of concern to arise may be whether the scene changes will be affected by the position of the off-stage lighting and sound equipment. Will the actor in his wheelchair be able to exit DSL as the masking marked on the ground plan does not allow enough room for the door to open and the chair to wheel out through a door closed by an unseen ASM standing behind it? Will the costume for the leading lady allow her to stretch up to light the candles on a chandelier? This problem actually occurred during work on a production of *War and Peace* by Leo Tolstoy when during the technical rehearsal it was discovered that the dress the actress was wearing did not allow for any broad arm movements; the dress had to be remade at extra cost and time, neither of which was really available. The important fact is that stage management never picked up and followed the issue through – all could have been avoided had the wardrobe been informed of the actress's movements during the early rehearsal period or at one of the progress meetings. The various departmental links are enormously important – no department can work in isolation and it is the job of the stage management to make sure that there is liaison. It is a good idea at these meetings for the stage management to bring along patterns of fabric for the covering of a piece of furniture or small props for the designer and director to see; this helps the stage management to know if they are working along the correct lines thus preventing the end result being unworkable or not to the designer's plans. There must be a ground plan laid out for reference and the model of the set design, providing it has not been dismantled to enable paintshop and workshop to check colour and design while building and painting. The prompt corner position needs to be established; in most theatres this is a movable object. The best position for the prompt desk needs to be decided. Despite the use of television monitors the DSM needs to see the stage and hear the actors.

OPPOSITE PAGE
An example of a rehearsal report.

'THE SNOWMAIDEN'

Rehearsal Report 9

Date: Thursday 1st February   Director: Stephen Medcalf
Venue: Lauderdale Tower B   D.S.M.:   Megan Phillips

General

1) During Act 1, (p.169) Mizgui (Mr Hakan Vramsmo) is picked up by most of the male chorus (10 people). He is in a horizontal spread-eagle position and the chorus are supporting him with their arms fully outstretched above their heads. They then turn in a circle with him still raised and lower him, feet first, DSC - he then pretends to have fallen.

Designer

1) See stage management note 1.
2) See workshop notes 1 and 2.

Stage Management

1) There are now only two wash jugs needed in the bath scene. The ones in rehearsals are not suitable as the director would like them to appear as china or porcelain, possibly with a design on them. To be confirmed with designer.
2) The number of sacks now needed is 14.

Workshop

1) The director would like to confirm that the head holes in the 'back wall' flat are above normal head height so that they are visible above the chorus. We may require small rostra or boxes to allow the cast to reach the head holes.
2) The head holes in the side flats will be at normal head height. We must remember that two cast members required to look through these holes are 5ft 4in and 5ft 6in and should not need a rostra to reach the holes.

There are no specific notes for props, paintshop, sound, LX and wardrobe.

Thank you

Sarah Morgan
Stage Manager

Cc: Stephen Medcalf, Isabella Bywater, Sophie Bugeaud, Simon Corder, Maxine Braham, Marion Marrs, Sue Thornton, Martin Hazlewood, Soozie Copley, John Phillips, Alex Madden, Karolina Norgate, Andy Wilson, Melissa Magna, Sue Hudson, Kate John, LX, Mark Newell, Steve Hawkins, Mark Richards, Megan Phillips, Gemma Tonge, Laura Streather, Clive Timms (24).

THE OFFICE AND REHEARSAL ROOM

It cannot be emphasized strongly enough that there needs to be a strong link between the stage management office and the rehearsal room. To keep this communication working efficiently it is necessary to use equipment such as mobile phones, pagers, E-mails and faxes. These must all be backed up by paperwork; the extremely useful production file must be in use all and every day. Competent use of the acquisition charts, scene availability charts, actors and creative team non-availability charts will make the day-to-day call sheets for rehearsals, wardrobe, music, movement, dance, and so on, much easier to organize. Daily use of the production file will also help you to keep track of letters to firms requesting information or the collation of research into the period. It will also mean that details about specialist advisers or chaperones for any children, or the production photographer and programme details can all be found in a central place.

It is useful to have some of the charts and all the call sheets on the office wall to make it easier to see this information quickly if you are on the telephone. The acquisitions chart and non-availability chart must be there, plus a calendar large enough to write the many daily events and important dates on. These dates would include that of the technical rehearsal and the pick-up dates for any hired items. The best materials to use for this calendar are the index file cards (used for the small box files); these cards come in three different sizes, the smallest version being the best. They are also produced in shades of white, blue, pink, yellow or green, useful for colour coding a show when the office walls are full of notices. If you use these cards you can add Post-it notes to them or turn them around if they are full. They can also be replaced if there is too much detail on them making them difficult to read. At the end of the show's run these cards should be collected and put into the production file.

The sign of an efficient stage manager is a tidy office and a tidy desk; it usually means their stage will be the same and the show is well thought through and organized.

STAGGER-THROUGHS

Stagger-throughs are early run-throughs of the whole play in the rehearsal room. It will be the first time the play has been put together in sequence since the read-through. To stagger means to stop when required and restart the section or scene, perhaps to discuss a different or easier way around a piece of action that worked in isolation but now is proving difficult in sequence.

All stage management must attend these stagger-throughs as it will give the team a better idea of how the show will work technically, where quick costume changes appear, if the scene changes will work to plan and the prop settings are appropriate. The stage management should set up the stage area in the rehearsal room and run the play as closely as possible to how it will be in a performance.

RUN-THROUGHS

Run-throughs are the early stages of a dress rehearsal, without the lights, set and full costume. It will be the next stage in the rehearsal process after the stagger-through. To run means not to stop unless the director thinks it is absolutely necessary. It is important for him to find out how things work in real time.

Stage management need to approach a run-through as if it were a performance. Some of the actual props and furniture are introduced into rehearsal replacing the stand-in items used in earlier rehearsals, especially if it is important to the action, for example a wheelchair, baby's pram, or a weapon. For the last couple of run-throughs you should make sure there are as many actual practical items as possible, such as working electrical goods, vacuum cleaners, transistor radios, tape recorders or CD players. Furniture or props that have to break or collapse on cue should also be provided as well as practical food and drink; as also sound and costume pieces, especially if there are some tricky changes, as it's the last time the cast and director have a chance to try out busy action before they reach the stage. By then it could be too late to make any major alterations.

Providing all Health and Safety requirements are met, and the rehearsal room is large enough, you may need to provide some important pieces of set, especially steel deck (rostra) for levels and treads (steps) for staircases.

Stage management should also make sure all props are set on the correct sides of the stage area, on neat and clearly laid out prop tables, with clearly marked areas for items that may appear from understage or are flown in. The DSM should be situated downstage below the setting line to time the show, prompt and cue any live or recorded sound. The stage manager should join them to make notes, orchestrate and help with the scene changes. The ASMs

should be on their allocated sides of the stage area, handing props out to the actors and receiving them as they come off, setting and striking props and furniture accordingly in the scene changes, producing live sound cues and operating the tape and or CD player. The run-throughs are also a chance for other staging departments to see the show and help them prepare for the production before everything transfers to the theatre. This will also allow more time for small changes to occur and the opportunity to iron out any potential difficulties.

Because a large audience of department staff and creative teams can be obtrusive in a small rehearsal room some directors will make sure they organize two or three run-throughs within the last week of rehearsals, allowing everyone to view the show in shifts. The staff needing to attend run-throughs are:

Creative Team
Director
Assistant Director
Sound Designer
Costume Designer
Lighting Designer.

A creative team in discussion around a model.

(Above) Choreographer Bill Deamer putting the company through a dance rehearsal.

Lighting designer John Roffey working on his plan.

OPPOSITE PAGE
(Top) Production manager Peter Johnson Booth checking on the design progress.

(Bottom) Wardrobe working on costumes in preparation for fittings.

If you were rehearsing a musical the creative team would also include:

Choreographer
Assistant Choreographer
Musical Director
Pianist/répétiteur.

Staging Departments
Production Manager
Company Stage Manager
Stage Manager
Deputy Stage Manager
Assistant Stage Managers
Wardrobe Mistress
Lx Head of Dept
Snd Head of Dept.

(Above) Stage management taking down a makeshift rostra in the rehearsal room.

Packed up to leave the rehearsal room.

TRANSFERRING ONTO THE STAGE

Stage management must be meticulous over this transfer, making sure that every measurement is noted on the ground plan. The rehearsal room often holds exact information, for example, the positions of furniture, pieces of set and specials (those specific spotlights for actors), and information on exits and entrances with enough room off-stage to accommodate the actor and their prop. The team need to treat the whole process as if they were on tour and use the same format as you would to pack at the end of a show that is transferring to the next venue. The transport could either be a van or a handcart depending on the size of the move and the distance to your theatre from the rehearsal room, but either way the transfer has to be thorough and careful in its execution.

You will need a box or tea chest for props with a list of its contents attached to the outside plus plenty of newspaper and bubble wrap for the breakables, for instance, china and glass. All sticks, umbrellas, pieces of wood should be tied in bundles. Delicate furniture should be covered and the cover secured making sure that nothing gets packed on top of it, with a polythene sheet over it if it is raining. The sound equipment, whether it's a couple of CD players or a complete system, needs to be thoroughly checked for all cables, extension leads and speakers. Make sure there are no odd shoes or handbags or other items of costume left behind. Comprehensive lists and a methodical approach to the task will ensure a successful transfer.

The rehearsal room itself must be checked for any stray piece of equipment, costumes or props that may be tucked away in a corner or under a chair. Remove all the marking tape from the floor and then thoroughly sweep and mop. Caretakers of rehearsal rooms are very particular and it's wise to keep on good terms with them. The kitchen area should be left clean with no empty or dirty milk bottles and cartons. Rubbish bags should be put in the outside dustbins, windows closed and all lights switched off before finally locking the door and returning to the theatre.

BACK AT THE THEATRE

You need to have previously organized a space with the production manager and any other member of the theatre staff; this can be either a small section of backstage behind the set of the current show, in the workshops, scenery dock or some alcove or partitioned-off area front of house that is neither seen nor dangerously impedes the thoroughfare of a member of the audience.

Usually stage management are running the show that is in performance while the rehearsals are in operation. The Saturday morning after the final run-through is when the transfer from the rehearsal room happens. As they will be involved in the matinée and evening show, none of the team will be able to unpack and check every individual item until sometime during the next day once the get-out (commonly known as the 'strike') has been completed. The 'strike'

means that the entire set is taken down, some of it is put away in the scenery store and some pieces are thrown away – especially if any of it is badly damaged, built in false perspective or at some odd angle and cannot be used again. The strike starts immediately after the final performance of the show on the Saturday night.

Once the 'strike' is completed everyone goes home for a much-needed sleep, and at some point on the Sunday afternoon or early evening the rehearsal room items are unpacked, checked and returned to the store if not being used, washed and cleaned and laid out in a dressing room at stage level or a corner of the wing area out of the technicians' way, then checked off scene by scene. All the furniture has the same treatment. Any work to be done by the stage management on a Sunday will be carefully organized, staggering the team's hours to make sure they only work one session of four hours otherwise there would be too much expense involved for weekend work. While an ASM deals with the props and furniture, the stage manager will be coping with various company calls for Monday, such as last-minute wardrobe and wig calls, press calls, rehearsal calls in another part of the theatre, names for the dressing room doors, updating the call board and making lists for the team to deal with first thing in the morning.

Once the weekend has passed and the set has been put up, the lighting designer and the electricians are about to start to focus all the lanterns. The stage management will transfer from the ground plan to the stage all the furniture marks (positions) and any marks for actors who will need a fixed point of light in which to stand or sit. These tightly focused areas are known as specials. This enables the lighting personnel to light where it is specifically required. These marks are crucial and often the director will be called for this session. It is also important for the SM to be around during the entire focus time, as apart from the DSM, they know the show better than anyone else.

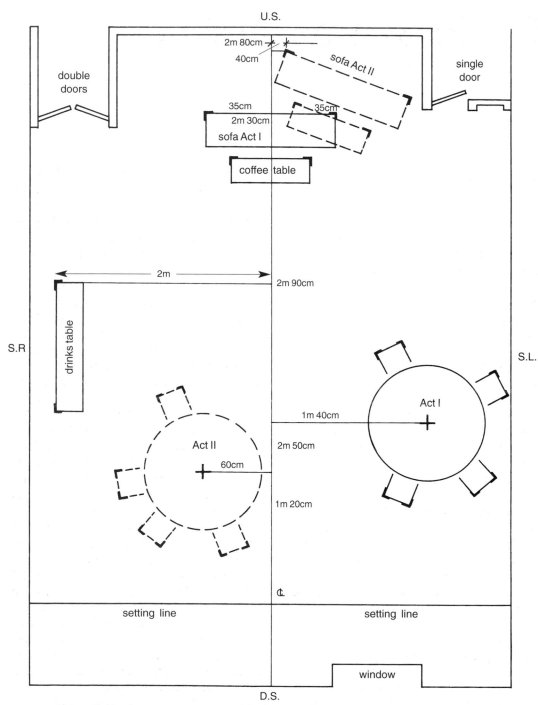

Measured marks for furniture positions taken from the rehearsal room.

7 PROP COLLECTING

RESEARCH

Research is an exciting part of the work of a stage management team. Interesting discoveries are made about authors, props and the way people of all nationalities lived and played in days gone by. You need to read the play thoroughly to find out about the storyline. As you turn each page you begin to know and understand the characters, why they talk and behave the way they do. You discover the author's meaning and that every prop is necessary and why it is important that the item is of a particular style, size or colour. You may find the play difficult because the characters are using strange expressions or handling props that are unfamiliar to you because the story is set in another country and in a period you know nothing about. Your point of research has started. If the play is set, for example, in a particular part of Australia in the late 1700s, make for the history books at the local library, take notes and find illustrations to enhance your notes, then start to make a picture storyboard for the rehearsal room and the stage management office. Before long you will have comprehensive information on the country, the period, their costume, home styles and the differences between rich and poor.

WORKING WITH THE DIRECTOR AND DESIGNER

Sometimes the director and designer decide to set the play in a different era from the one in which the author has written it, bringing everything into the modern day. You will still need to study the play and collect research in both the original and modern period to help the company, director and yourselves to understand what is meant by phrases and props no longer in use today.

Once you have made a list from the script of all props, furniture and dressings, you will have filled in several pages of the acquisitions chart. The stage manager would organize a meeting with the designer and director before the start of rehearsals and hopefully before the first production meeting, however this is not always possible because of the creative team's commitments. You and your team should have the acquisitions chart, script, research material (storyboard), books of reference illustrations and any notes you have with you at this meeting, the designer will also have some of their own research material. The director may also be in on these meetings. If not, then a meeting will be organized by the stage management at a later date. A great deal of information will also arise from the rehearsal process.

In the discussion the listed props are talked through item by item, although it is usually not necessary to spend time on things such as a man's or lady's handkerchief, pieces of paper, letters, and so on, because the script will be self-explanatory coupled with the initiative of the stage management to gather these together accordingly. However, if it's for specifics, such as, colour, shape and size of cushions, curtains, sofas, chairs, babies and their prams, suitcases, and so on, then these items will be discussed in detail. By the end of the meeting you should have a comprehensive set of notes and drawings to guide you along the right lines and help you to know what you are searching for. Throughout the searching process, stage management must update the designer if they need to deviate from the original idea because it is too difficult to find or acquire. However, this must not turn into what almost amounts to harassment of the designer, because the ASM is constantly phoning up to ask whether the box requested would be all right if it's a fraction larger than asked for or the shade of blue is somewhat paler than the original request. This is why as many questions as possible are asked at that early meeting, and stage management should use their initiative. To illustrate this point, an ASM once made nine visits to the rehearsal room to ask the director about a prop and used up the designer's fax paper roll asking the same questions. Neither of the creative team members was very pleased at the constant barrage of questions. The prop mentioned in the script

A Modern Substitute for a Period Prop

The period is 1888 and the character is knitting a man's sock on four bone needles. It is impossible to find actual needles of that era. However, you can buy fine light cream-coloured wooden needles for knitting socks, and dark grey wool, that does not look as if it is nylon! Do not use coloured plastic or metal needles and light or bright coloured nylon or wool mixture.

was a medal attached to a blue-striped ribbon; was there no more detail about the type of medal or the size? What was it made of? How and where it was worn? The width of the ribbon? The width of the stripes? The number of stripes? The shades of blue? All these questions could have been answered at the first meeting and by reading the script thoroughly, as it later became apparent to the ASM that the answer lay in the text.

More meetings will be arranged, this time with the stage management to retrace their steps by working down the acquisitions chart, picking out the priorities, usually starting with difficult tricky items that everyone knows will be expensive and often unattainable.

The stage manager should then allocate to each of the ASMs a list of props to find or acquire by a certain time each day, which will ensure that future deadlines are met. If you are pounding the local high street borrowing and buying props, do make sure a comprehensive list is made and that the ASMs are not making unnecessary visits to shops and stores or having to repeat visits when the list could have been dealt with in one go. Do not forget to buy cleaning materials for those tarnished silver items and china and glasses to be washed, such as silver polish, furniture polish, washing up liquid, tea towels, dish mops, dusters and so on,

Examples of Props Requiring Priority Attention

A period wheelchair, when can it be in rehearsal? Is it possible to have a false armrest mounted on it containing a remote control for the television?

A rehearsal tape of the sound of gunfire

A teapot that has to have just the spout broken off when it is dropped

A local regional newspaper with a specific headline in the year 1936

These items would need to be addressed immediately as they could take some time to acquire

all of which will be required prior to the technical rehearsal. As preparations for the show progresses, you will hear from the rehearsal room various snippets of information as to what is happening to the props you have been diligently collecting – the silver tray borrowed from the local silversmith gets thrown across the stage during the action of a tense scene, the period newspaper costing several pounds per copy is to be torn up during each performance and the flimsy, hired period chair is jumped onto by a 13-stone actor. Once you have checked the text for any references to such action you need to talk to the DSM to try and find out exactly how the scene is performed, and if possible to attend the rehearsal when the scene is being played to find out for yourself what is going on. If you are worried by the action you see in the rehearsal room you should discuss this with the director to reach an alternative solution. This may mean contacting the designer as the director has suggested using a cheap replica of the tray so it would be possible to have a new one for each performance, the newspaper could be made up by the stage management and photocopied, there could then be one made for each show, and a different sturdier chair could be hired, able to take the weight of the 13-stone actor jumping on it. The designer may not agree with the director on this matter and yet another alternative may need to be thought of. This may require your tact and diplomatic skills with the designer and the director plus an artistic eye for adapting stock items and seeing how you can make cheap things look expensive.

This is where you need a good eye to see the possibility of using a chair from the prop room that could be modified, making it strong enough for use in the plotted action. Talk to the DSM to try and find out exactly how the scene is performed. Plans should be made to pound the local high street in search of charity shops for those much required items no longer of value to their last owners. From a silver teapot or crystal water jug to grandad's pipe rack and tobacco jar. The thrill when you find the sought-for item is terrific.

WHERE TO LOOK

The other places to try and find cheap old-fashioned props are car boot sales, garden fêtes and church bazaars. It is unlikely that you will always find exactly what you are looking for, but you need to be able to see the possibilities in something that will be approved by the eagle eyes of the designer and director.

Back-street junk on the pavement in front of a shop. This is a stage manager's goldmine.

(Above) A good selection of furniture and smaller items. A good place for a browse.

(Above) The friendly antiques shop which may be willing to lend.

(Left) A street of second-hand furniture shops saves time. Always have details of heights, widths and so on, to eliminate items when you are faced with a selection.

WHAT TO LOOK FOR

For a production of Noel Coward's *Blithe Spirit*, the designer wanted all props furniture and dressings to be pure Art Deco. To achieve this by buying the items would have cost a small fortune, but after several days of discussion amongst themselves the stage management went to all the car boot sales and markets they could find, and bought two authentic Art Deco cigarette boxes for the princely sum of five pounds for the two. Exhausted and with nowhere else to look, the stage management went on a tour of local cut-price gift shops, the city's major department store, and Woolworths. They ended up finding many vases, ornaments, bowls, cocktail glasses and a soda siphon that were all reproduction art deco. On top of the discovery, they were able to acquire all these items on loan for the duration of the show in return for a programme credit and complimentary tickets.

(Above) Various items of silver. These may well be too expensive to buy but are useful for research or the owner may be willing to lend them.

Period newspapers are expensive and sometimes hard to find. If you come across inexpensive ones, it is always worth buying them for your props store.

Programme Credits

Companies and individuals donating items for a production are usually credited in the following way:

We would like to thank the following for their kind assistance:
Wheelchair by B.R.Smith.
Continental trunk and set of suitcases by T. Brown & Co.
Silver coffee pot by Hamptons Silversmiths.
Small occasional table by Mrs Lock of Betty's Tea Rooms.

PROPERTIES LOANS FORM

PRODUCTIONS:

_____

ON LOAN FROM:

PHONE No: CONTACT: _____
DATE: _____

_____

ITEMS plus VALUES:

_____

COLLECTED BY:

ISSUED BY:

TO BE RETURNED DURING THE WEEK OF :

A prop borrowing form. The conditions of borrowing and lending are usually printed on the back.

Once everything had been taken back to the theatre, there was the fussy task of carefully taking all labels and bar codes off the items. It is important to keep all tickets and labels safely and put them back on all the goods at the end of the run. Always return borrowed props in the same condition as you received them or better. This usually guarantees that you can borrow again in the future and it shows that you are careful and reliable.

TATTING AND TARTING

The definition of the word *tatting* is the art of making lace; it also means shabby clothing, and to tat up is to make something look less shabby, which is why stage management use the term for turning second-hand props or furniture into beautiful period items.

Tarting is probably a word made up by stage manage-

Finding just the right prop.

of their list of priorities, therefore the task would usually fall to the stage management team. Many regional theatres cannot afford to run a props department so it is usually a foregone conclusion that stage management pool their artistic skills and make all the small personal and hand props, and certainly do the *tatting* and *tarting*. A lot of these small props would be stock items or you would buy them (as cheaply as possible) and then add the required decorative design. Do not decorate borrowed items unless the owner has given permission for you to do so.

Do not spend money on real silver or gold pieces, use metals such as gilt or chrome or any other form of cheap metals, they look like the real thing when on stage, sometimes better once they are amongst other props and enhanced by the lighting.

ment many years ago, to describe dressing (or 'overdressing') a prop by using a lot of trim and sparkle and colour, to make or add to a decorative design. Personal props, such as cigarette cases, holders, lighters, matchboxes, wallets, purses, compacts and so on can be made into the correct style by drawing or painting on to the object a decorative period pattern. If the prop were a box of biscuits or chocolates you would give the box the same artwork treatment.

However, if there is no artistic talent within the stage management team and you have a props department, they may be able to assist stage management with what is required. This kind of request, for an already overworked props department would be of minor importance to them, time consuming, and possibly put at the bottom

An ASM making a 1930s soap flakes packet.

87

The soap flake packet nearing completion.

Modern Packaging

Be careful if you use modern boxes. Not only have logos changed but also the package sizes are very different today, generally being larger than their period counterparts. Also be careful of metric weights printed on the side and the modern bar code.

Some of the large and more complex pieces of furniture are more likely to be hired from a theatrical firm in London. Even if you are working in the regional theatres the designers often hire furniture, costume and wigs from a London firm.

Some London Hire Firms

The current addresses and telephone numbers for these firms should be checked with directory enquiries.

Props and Furniture
Royal National Theatre
Superhire
Studio & TV Hire
Farley Hire
A & M Hire

Silverware
Lewis & Kaye (Hire) Ltd

Weapons
Bapty's
Rent-A-Sword (Alan Meek)

HIP BATH

Trading Post

Trading Post

Dimensions:

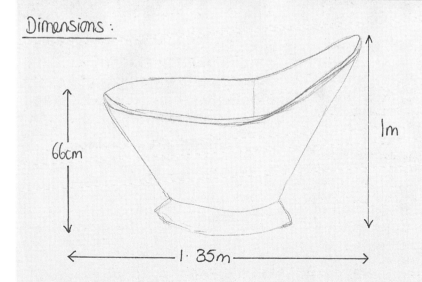

66cm

1m

1·35m

Cream finish.

A hired hip bath. A polaroid snapshot was taken at the hire company and the bath sketched and annotated by the ASM to give better details once they had returned to base.

A hired coffee pot of a particularly unusual design. As a stage manager, you must develop an eye for spotting such items as you go about propping.

The stage manager must always try and travel with the designer when they hire goods. This is to ensure the designer does not get carried away with dressing the set and overspend on the budget. They also need to make sure that the items chosen are practical for the action within the production, for example that the sofa will take being jumped on or have food thrown over it, the back is low enough to lean on or climb over, the arms can be sat on or have a cup of tea balanced on them.

THE MAKING OF LARGE AND SPECIALIST PROPS

An example of a large or specialist prop would be an item far too complex for the stage management to make or perhaps to find, such as a chair that has to be picked up and smashed to the floor or against a wall. Or a table that tilts just enough to allow props to slide slowly down to the table's edge. Perhaps pieces of furniture that have to be anti-raked to allow them to look and be used as normal on a raked (sloped) stage. Maybe a bed that has to fly in to the stage with a person sitting on it or a toy donkey that has to explode, only to be returned in its original state

for the next act. The list often seems long and complex. These items would be made by your props department if you had one or by an outside firm. There would need to be initial discussions concerning the details of how it will work, what the priorities are with the designer and the director and if possible the stage manager should also be present. There would need to be involvement with the workshop, electricians and the staging departments, as the props or piece of furniture would affect their set or set pieces or the wiring up of a pyrotechnic explosion. You would need to keep the prop maker up to date with any changes to the prop during the rehearsal process and vice versa.

FOODSTUFFS
(WHISK IT AND MIX IT)

There is always food and drink needed in a production, whether it is a one-man show or has a cast of thirty. The production can be a drama, comedy, opera, musical or a revue, there will always be something to eat or drink from a sweet and a glass of water to an eight-course dinner with a glass of drink for each course. To be able to perform and eat at the same time can be quite difficult and stressful to an actor and singer. With the influence of film and television the directors tend to want to use the real food listed in the script. This is usually totally impractical.

Real Food often Requested for the Stage

Dinner party with roast meat, gravy and vegetables
Fruit pie or trifles
A small feast of gruel
Porridge
Bread and milk
Chowder

THE IMPORTANCE
OF PREPARATION

A stage manager must make sure the actor is not allergic to certain foods, such as anything with a nut or wheat content, or if anyone is diabetic. You should try to make a list when collecting contact numbers from your company

---

Why Some Dishes Are Impractical

- Roast beef on a meat dish (uncut) is expensive; you may need a new joint every performance once it was cut into because the action asks for the roast to be straight from the oven.
- It would be difficult to keep and you would need to find access to a fridge.
- Keeping uncooked meat is not easy or safe and it can become contaminated travelling from the shop to the fridge.
- The meat is not easy to cook, you would need access to an oven close to the stage, and time to cook it, and the correct time to serve it as though it was straight from the oven.
- Many people have valid reasons for not eating meat.
- The pastry crust of a fruit pie is not easy for the actors to eat, the filling will be very hot (as pastry holds the heat) when it is brought from the oven, the pastry is dry and crumbly and an actor may choke as they try to speak.
- A trifle has to be kept firm and cool and therefore access to a fridge is necessary. If it needs to be renewed for each performance a ready-made one is expensive, and to make one can be messy and time-consuming and there are always the days when the jelly and custard do not work!
- Gruel, porridge, bread and milk are all items of food that are difficult to keep fresh and looking as if they had just been made when brought on stage.
- Gruel and porridge congeal, and bread and milk become very sloppy and pappy.
- Chowder is a type of fish soup. Using any form of fish on stage is dangerous, as it tends to go off more easily than other foodstuffs.
- Not everyone can eat fish and some people are allergic to it and in particular any form of seafood.

on the first day of rehearsals. Do make sure you read the play thoroughly to find out what food is required. This makes planning easier, and you are then able to suggest safe alternatives for those company members who have any dietary problems. Always make sure your preparation area is clean and tidy. The work surface must be covered with a plastic cloth, have a chopping board, mixing bowls and the necessary knives, forks and spoons, as you would have in your own kitchen (only a smaller selection), access to a sink with hot and cold water, an electrical socket and the use of an electric kettle and a small fridge. A microwave oven is a luxury you may not always be able to acquire, unless the green room is fully equipped. However, it may be possible to persuade the chef in your theatre restaurant to let you use his cooker for half an hour. Also have plenty of cooking foil and clingfilm for covering the food when prepared, theatres are notoriously dusty. Covering up all edible items prevents actors having nibbles as they pass the prop tables. For one production the stage management picked up a tray containing plates of grapes, cubes of cheese, biscuits and small sandwiches to set in the scene change only to find the plates empty except for one, on which lay a sad-looking bare grape stalk.

FOOD MENUS

There are a number of alternatives to the real thing that stage management can provide that will still look like the meat and vegetable dish asked for in the text along with a fine wine or liqueur to accompany it. The idea is to make the meal as palatable for the performer as possible, to prevent choking or gagging on mouthfuls of food especially if they have to eat quickly or stuff it all into their mouths before delivering a four-minute speech or singing a song.

Healthfood shops sell various items that look like meat, usually soya; with lots of salad or

---

Points to Remember when Preparing Food for the Stage

Requirements of the Play
Period of the play
Particular events, for example, a wedding or Christmas feast
Particular circumstances, for example wartime (of any date)
Circumstances of the characters, for example wealthy or poor

Requirements of the Actors
Allergies
Religious or moral beliefs
Acting while eating while speaking

Preparation Problems
Availability of a clean preparation area
Availability of cooking appliances, for example, ovens or microwave
Suitable storage space, for example, fridge, enough wing space

Solutions
Smash
Baby foods
Fruit
Salads
Vegetables

---

vegetables to dress the dish this can be very effective. Should you want a joint of ham or beef or perhaps a whole chicken or turkey, then a fake one is made with a hollow space; into this space is placed already sliced soya meat that the actor can appear to carve if this is the action required.

If the food is only looked or picked at, perhaps thrown around the stage, then Smash (potato powder) mixed to the consistency required to sculpture into the necessary shapes is very useful. Smash can produce anything you wish to put your artistic talents to, for example, fish, scrambled egg, fried eggs, sausages, burgers, chicken pieces or small joints.

You also have to think of the speed at which an actor has to eat and speak at the same time, often with complex action added.

Fruit is another option. Banana is a favourite; it can be made into steak or bacon, diced and sliced for carrots or courgettes. It is simple to use and eat and full of vitamins! Apples can be made into chips, peeled and sliced into chip shapes, left to go brown with some help from food colouring or burnt sugar, and when bitten into, the inside is white as a chip would be.

Baby foods are another tasty and easy way to digest food, especially for period shows with a peasant or army flavour to the play, and when gruel is required, the rice, semolina, or milky rice dishes are ideal. Apple purée is excellent for

Preparing food for the stage from powdered mashed potato and food colouring.

Prepared food: chips, courgettes, chops, as well as various drinks. All prepared with powdered potato and food colouring.

Food in performance. Some of this is real and some fake. It helps to make the fake food appear real if the food on the plate is edible.

oysters in their (well-washed) shells from the fishmonger. Instant whips or the equivalent are also easy and digestible. These can be made to look good in a dish or bowl as stew or gruel.

If it is difficult to find out-of-season fruits and vegetables, it is possible to turn to tinned or frozen goods. Some actors will insist on the real thing, and therefore stage management need to look carefully into the menu as some foods are easy for an actor to choke on, setting off a bout of coughing that makes it difficult for them to speak. Try and steer clear of nuts, dry cake or biscuits and crusty bread. When the script demands this and there is no alternative, always have a glass or jug of water somewhere on the set. Try not to fill a sandwich with all the listed content (unless there is no alternative!).

Keep to just the fats, margarine, butter or a health spread. Keep the slices small and crusts cut off making them easier to eat. However, there are texts that demand everything on the menu in great detail, in which case these suggestions would not be appropriate.

WINES AND SPIRITS

If you provided real bottles of wines and spirits, then the performers would be very drunk by the end of the show. It would also encourage those performers who are fond of their drink. One elderly actor who loved his drink, held a secret between the stage manager and himself, in which his brandy glass always contained real brandy; it was placed on stage already poured, usually replaced with another in the interval change. Because it was a secret between the stage manager and the actor the ASM knew nothing of this. When the curtain came down on the first act, she went on stage after the stage manager had refilled the glass with the last drop from the actor's brandy bottle, collected the dirty glasses from the stage including the glass of real brandy and washed them up for the next act!

NON-ALCOHOLIC DRINK FOR THE STAGE

Period beer or ale did not have a head (that froth at the top of a glass). This came over to England when the American imports arrived.

So it makes it easy for stage management when it is a period play, to find a substitute. This would be tap water and a very small drop of burnt sugar solution. Burnt sugar can be bought from most large leading chemists at the dispensary counter. It really is burnt sugar and the original is a thick, dark brown, treacle-like substance, looking a bit like molasses, and is used for colouring some medicines. When purchased, the product has already been diluted several times and is less like treacle, more just a dark brown liquid. It is then diluted many times but two drops from a pipette into a jug of water will be enough to make the water look like the whisky or brandy intended. Because it has been diluted so much there is absolutely no taste at

Food and drink in performance. Mephisto, *Guildhall School of Music and Drama, Director Wyn Jones, Designer Sara Blenkensop, Lighting Designer Bruno Poet.* Photo: Laurence Burns

Food and drink in performance. Note this food was actually consumed. **Mephisto, Guildhall School of Music and Drama, Director Wyn Jones, Designer Sara Blenkensop, Lighting Designer Bruno Poet.** *Photo: Laurence Burns*

all. Over a decade ago, cold tea and gravy browning were used, which did taste quite disgusting and used to turn many a stomach.

Other drinks can be achieved by adding food colourings to the burnt sugar or used on their own with soft drinks added to make the taste more appealing, especially when an actor has to drink glass upon glass or a full bottle. For those thick drinks, use a milk drink you are able to whisk. For the play *Born in the Gardens* one of the characters is passionate about Advocaat often known as eggnog! It is a sweet thick yellow Dutch liqueur made of raw egg yolks and brandy. The character drank this all the way through the play and it was constantly referred to. Milk-shake was used with the favourite flavour of banana and a little extra yellow food colouring.

The various cordial firms will donate free bottles of soft drinks, both fizzy and still. Coca-Cola are extremely helpful and generous and when asked will often help with period packaging. Schweppes are also helpful with all mixers.

Moet et Chandon and Veuve Cliquot are also helpful and will send sealed bottles of stage champagne (ginger ale) that will pop when opened. Pernod is represented by coloured water, adding Robinsons Lemon Barley Water to make it cloudy.

Tea and coffee are usually the real thing and milk can be soya, powdered or fresh depending on the request. Remember to use leaf tea with period productions (tea bags were introduced in 1952), with cubed or granulated sugar according to period.

96

8 SEEING AND HEARING

NOISES OFF

Despite the latest technology, live sound and visual effects arc still used, either to enhance a recorded or mechanical effect or in their own right because the sound gives a better intensity of noise or suits the mood of a production. On occasions live effects can be the saving of a show should all power shut down during a performance. A director will often ignore the tremendous variety of sound the new equipment of today can produce, and ask for the old-fashioned basics for his show.

As mentioned in the chapter about stage props, often the most successful items are those made larger than life that to the naked eye seem crude and unrealistic but put on stage in context and under the lights they look fantastic. This can also apply to sound effects. However good the mechanics of a great sound system are, the sound of a live door slamming off in the wings after an actor rushes from the stage in a supposed temper is so much more realistic, especially if the actor has had to operate the effect themselves with a small door built into a wooden box. Apart from the sound, timing is involved and the way the actor handles the door and that is often the effect that needs to reach the audience.

A small door in a frame complete with handles, locks and bolts attached is ideal. It should be free-standing (or preferably lying on its back on the ground) to be slammed by the actor when they come off stage or by a member of stage management. This door could also be mounted onto a box to enable a different sound

from the free-standing one. The alternatives are a 70–75cm long batten of wood, padded at one end for variation of effect or striking a hammer on the stage floor or on a box or off-stage pass door. This can produce quite a dramatic door knock as if on a heavy castle door.

If the effect calls for a heavy castle door with bolts and chains the sound system is the best way of handling the correct type and depth of noise. In the days before the new systems, all noises from castle doors to trains rumbling past were done live from the wings with a complex collection of wooden crates, metal sheets, chains and actual bolts on a piece of board, plus, of course, many crew members. Sometimes these effects were used on their own or backed up by the old system of the turntable and several 78 records of train noises and so on. The grooves on the records of the soundtrack required, were marked with a chinagraph pencil in white or yellow, and the specially weighted needle head dropped on to this turning recorded on cue, then the noise interspersed with the crackling of the 78 would be fed through speakers set in an appropriate place on stage. Even with the production of cassette tapes and CDs there would often be a back-up of live effects, not perhaps with the same collection of hardware and personnel. But it somehow gave the correct feeling and depth to the noise asked for, with the addition of better timing from the actors and stage management, making for good teamwork.

Having modern sound systems comprising mini discs and samplers, does not mean that

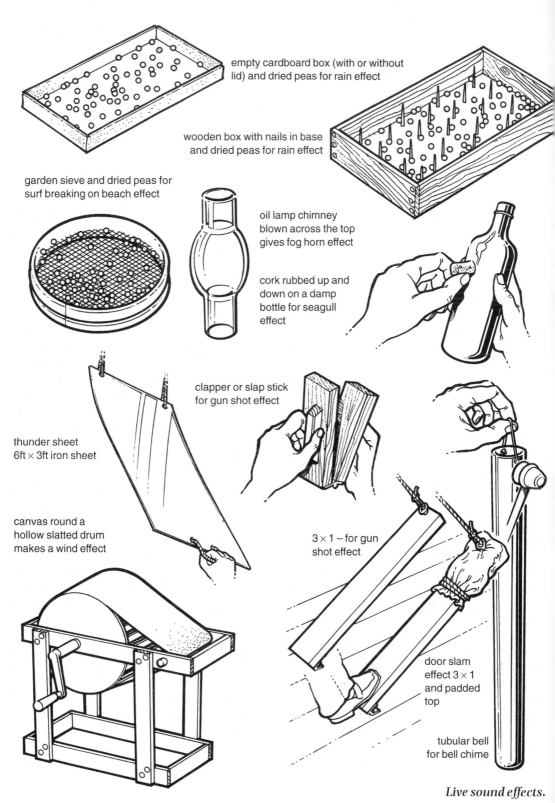

empty cardboard box (with or without lid) and dried peas for rain effect

wooden box with nails in base and dried peas for rain effect

garden sieve and dried peas for surf breaking on beach effect

oil lamp chimney blown across the top gives fog horn effect

cork rubbed up and down on a damp bottle for seagull effect

clapper or slap stick for gun shot effect

thunder sheet 6ft × 3ft iron sheet

canvas round a hollow slatted drum makes a wind effect

3 × 1 – for gun shot effect

door slam effect 3 × 1 and padded top

tubular bell for bell chime

Live sound effects.

directors cannot back up the recorded noise for their production with live effects.

The Thunder Sheet

This is a metal sheet approximately one metre wide and two metres long with a handle on the bottom edge, suspended in an upstage wing area. The sheet is shaken on cue and will represent the distant and close thunder rumbles and ultimate crack, that you often hear in a bad storm. The electrics department would provide the necessary visual effects of sheet and forked lighting.

The Wind Machine

This is a wooden drum, the sides of the drum being slatted rather than solid as in a normal drum. The slatted drum is mounted into two wooden shafts with a handle protruding at one end to enable it to be turned clock- or anti-clockwise. A piece of scenic canvas is attached firmly along one side of the wooden mount, taken over the drum and hung loosely with a wooden batten in the end to weight the canvas. When the handle is turned the drum rotates, the slats rub against the canvas, and the sound it produces is like the whining whoosh of blowing wind. The depth of sound can be alternated by fast or slow rotation or in sudden bursts.

Rain Effect

This effect can be mingled with the two earlier effects (thunder-sheet and wind machine) or used on its own. The sound of rain beating on the roof of a house or in the trees often needs to be very specifically timed to speech or action. For this sound you need a large shallow cardboard box 1m long by 50cm wide with a lid, inside which you place a handful of dried pulses such as chickpeas, dried peas and, depending on the sound required, split peas. You then rotate the box around by hand and the contents will rattle and race over the bottom of the box sounding like raindrops. After practice you learn to rotate smoothly and in a continuous movement.

Should you need to have a different type of sound, a good tip is to line the box with polythene or paper and you will hear a different type of pitter-patter. You could use a wooden box with nails hammered through the bottom producing spikes in the base of the box, the contents will then have an irregular rhythm when rotated. This box could be mounted on a wooden stand and tilted instead of rotated by hand. Similar action with dried peas rotated around a garden sieve would make the sound of waves gently breaking on a shore. This latter device does not need a lid.

GENERAL NOISES OFF

Glass Crash

The large crash of a body falling through a greenhouse or large closed window can be achieved by having a pile of broken glass and a smaller amount in a bucket, then on cue you tip the load from the bucket onto the pile; this action is then quickly followed by some stage braces wrapped in an old blanket which makes a good sound of a falling body. Another glass smashing sound is the action of tipping one bucket of glass into another.

Great care must be taken with this effect. Use strong gardening gloves and plastic eye shields. Keep all persons except the operator well away from the designated area, making sure the pile of glass and buckets are on a large piece of hardboard, old floor cloth or plastic sheet. Replacing the glass with broken china and pieces of metal can make a similar crash effect.

Gunshots

Gunshots can be achieved as for the door slam with a wooden batten without the padded end (unless you want the thud of a silencer). The old-fashioned heavy-duty football rattles can be used for machine-gun fire. When the sound totally failed one night on a production of *The Long and the Short and the Tall* which takes place in the Burma jungle during the Second World War, the stage management leapt into action and not only made animal jungle noises with their mouths but grabbed pieces of wood and the rattles they had standing by for such an emergency and made the battle noises for the end of one of the scenes. According to various reports at the end of the evening, many members of the audience were heard to say that the play was excellent and very realistic especially the battle scene – they knew as they had been there in 1942!

Firing a starting pistol into an empty dustbin can make the sound of a loud and deep gunshot of a much heavier weapon. All these live effects for guns can also be a good stand-by for those practical weapons that always seem to malfunction when fired by an actor on stage. The stage management have to be alert and quick off the mark, as there will be the click-click of the gun on stage, a long pause, then the slap of wood from the wings! You can have a stand-by gun in the wings too, but as yet, it has never worked one hundred per cent; each time the on-stage gun has failed so has the stand-by gun – the favourite choice of most directors is the piece of wood!

Bells

There are many different effects from different types of bells. The tolling bell of a monastery or convent can be achieved using a tubular bell struck with a padded wooden beater or stick, either on the top of the tubular bell or on its side depending on the specific sound you may require. The same tubular bell can be used for a mantle clock by using a metal stick; this gives a tinkly sound as opposed to the deep resonance of the padded wooden stick. There are of course different notes for these tubular bells, the most useful being a G. The sound of a school or ship's bell, servant's bell or old-fashioned doorbell is best produced using a hand bell. These can be mounted on a board by a coiled spring (as the old shop-door bells) or attached on a stand so it can be rung by a chord tied to the clanger. There are different-sized hand bells and it may be

necessary to acquire a certain size for the effect needed. For a telephone bell or doorbell there are various-sounding electric bells that can be wired to a board near the phone position or actually on a front door (on the set) with a lead running back to the prompt desk. The director may want the actors to ring their own bell that would therefore be connected to a battery. The type of phone bell can usually be acquired from the archives of British Telecom. You would need to research the type of phone bell, depending on the period as single rings became double rings in England although some areas still use single rings – trim phones, American phones, European phones and so on, all have a specific sound.

Pops and Squeaks

These can be achieved using a bicycle pump adapted to take a bottle cork on a length of string, making it work as a pop gun for the popping of champagne corks. Damp corks rubbed up and down a bottle sound like the sad cry of a seagull. Cellophane scrunched in the hands sounds like the crackle of fire, and bubble wrap supplies the pops. All this can be enhanced when scrunched in front of a microphone.

Horses' Hooves

Two halves of an empty coconut shell played together in the right tempo reproduces the sound of a horse walking, trotting or at a gallop. Add small bells to your wrist to give the sound of a horse and sleigh.

VISUAL EFFECTS

Rain (Wet and Dry)

For a production set in the garden of a large colonial house on an island in the South Seas, a heavy rainfall was required with characters running in and out getting soaked. The designer and production manager came up with the idea of using a loop of metal piping suspended from a flying bar. This piping had holes

Visual effects.

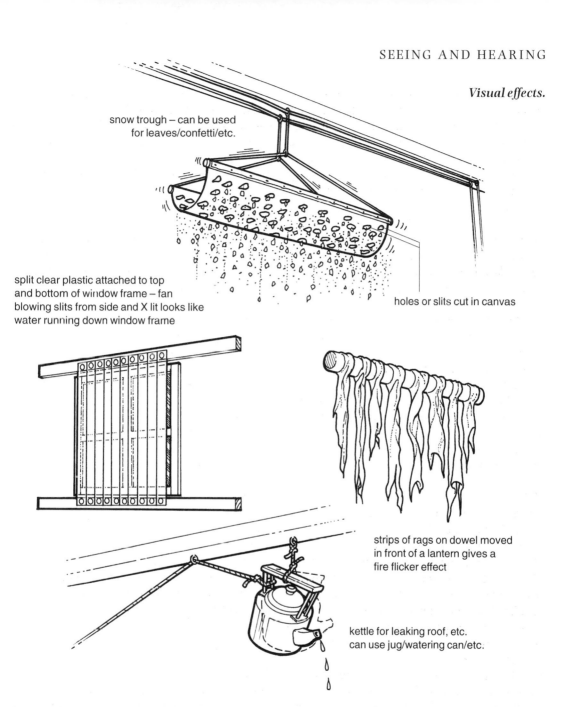

snow trough – can be used
for leaves/confetti/etc.

split clear plastic attached to top
and bottom of window frame – fan
blowing slits from side and X lit looks like
water running down window frame

holes or slits cut in canvas

strips of rags on dowel moved
in front of a lantern gives a
fire flicker effect

kettle for leaking roof, etc.
can use jug/watering can/etc.

punched into it rather like the rose of a watering can, there was a tank and small garden pond pump, and a trough under the piping to catch the water that ran back into the tank, the pump pushed the water up to the perforated piping, the drops fell through the holes and there were real wet rain drops! The effect when lit was terrific. However the cost was high, space was tricky and there was the daily maintenance of the piping and the pump.

Another way of achieving the above without using water, except to sprinkle the actors with when they ran on and off stage, was to use a rice drop and cross lighting. Take several pounds of uncooked white long-grain rice, put into a box or trough-like bag with slits, suspend this from a flying bar, with a sash line to the wings or fly floor. Place on stage painted scenic canvas or polythene sheet that will help contain the fallen grains of rice. On the cue for rain the line off to the wings or fly floor should be jiggled about, shaking the bag or box and releasing the rice through the holes. When cross-lit with the stage lights the rice looks like drops of water, the noise of it falling on the stage (especially on plastic) sounds like the pitter-patter of rain. This system of rice was used in a production of *Faust* with the addition of a little water and you could not tell the difference; the water was used at the very front of the stage and the rice was used from centre stage to the back. You must be careful not to use the water and rice absolutely together; otherwise you could have a lumpy pudding forming on the set.

If you only need to see raindrops on the window of your set, and the backstage space is limited a simple way to make the effect of raindrops is to attach a sheet of plastic tightly to the top and bottom of the window frame and with a sharp knife slit the plastic top to bottom at half inch intervals. Place a small table-top fan to one side and cross-light – the plastic will ripple as the fan blows and with the light trained on it will look like rain drops running down the window.

Falling Snow

This can be achieved by using the same method as the rice bag; only the rice would be substituted with small paper flakes. Because of the strict fire regulations care must be taken with anything made of paper. One can obtain specially made snowflakes from paper that has been treated with fireproofing. It is quite expensive, so make sure that you are able to reuse the flakes after each show. Many different firms deal with

this, not necessarily from one central area – often you are able to find a contact in your local town or city, particularly if you have a TV or film studio nearby. Salt is another type of snow effect, but it has to be used sparingly and carefully as it can make the stage extremely slippery.

Dancing Flames (Shadows)

The cosy look of shadows of dancing flames on the walls of a room when the lights are out can also have sinister meaning in a thriller, or if you need the effect of a burning building outside the window of a house. Or as in a TV programme on the history of music, there was a scene from an opera showing the mouth of the devil's cave. The mouth of the cave consisted of an arched opening with the rest of the cave presented in perspective, the result looking as if it was the entrance to a deep flame-ridden abyss. The crew each had a stick about 30cm long with varying lengths of fabric strips attached. They placed these in front of studio floor lanterns each inserted with a red filter – on cue the technicians waggled these sticks of fabric strips and the effect of the flaming mouth of hell was achieved. Simple, cheap and effective.

Blood

This can be a nightmare for the wardrobe department and stage management, particularly with hired items such as elaborate costumes or a beautiful cream velvet-covered sofa and deep-pile white rug. Bottles of stage blood are made to come out of fabric when washed or cleaned. Usually this happens, however there will always be some fabrics that do not wash or clean well; it may depend on how the blood has been mixed or diluted, and what effect needed to be achieved. If it has to be a deep red thick flow of blood from a stab wound or perhaps a blow to the head, the director will probably not want it diluted at all. Usually stage management and wardrobe get together with samples of the blood and fabrics and practise until they are able to come up with a workable recipe. Very often children's finger-paint can be used as it is non-toxic, washes out of clothing and is a lot cheaper. The film and stage blood costs over £20 for quite a small bottle; it is reasonably economical, but that does depend on the length of your play's run and the number of performances you do.

There are special types of blood that are non-toxic and can be used for the face, eyes and mouth or for wounds on other parts of the body. Do make sure you have the correct type for your particular effect, as it could be harmful. You should be able to purchase the blood from most theatrical costumiers.

For stabbing and gunshots, it is a case of making up a blood bag and attaching this to the actor. When the bag is pierced with a dagger or sword the blood will seep from the bag onto the clothing of the actor. It is well known both in film, TV and stage that the best type of blood bag is made from a condom; it is more reliable in every way than a child's balloon or polythene bag.

If a gunshot wound is needed a bag is attached to the body in the same way as you would for a stabbing, but this time with a mechanism of string tying the bag closed, the string is fed along the arm of the actor who would, when shot, pull the string and release the blood making it look as if the bullet had entered his body. There is not necessarily any one way of dealing with these effects, each set of stage management and actors will find and invent their own methods. A props master can also be very helpful with effects like these, sometimes taking responsibility for the device. Health and safety is also a consideration as far as the methods you use are concerned. Make sure the method you use is safe, for instance the backing for blood bags will take the stabbing of a knife or sword blade without penetrating the actor or that the blood used on the actor's face or near the eyes and mouth is the correct type of blood suitable for use near that part of the body.

SCENE CHANGES: PRINCIPLES AND PRACTICE

The stage management must forward plan all scene changes. They must be worked out thoroughly rather like a military exercise. Despite all the modern technical facilities a lot of theatres have – that is, lifts, motorized flying and

(Left) Toxic and non-toxic blood and blood capsules.
(Above) Perfecting the wounds.

103

trucks – there are still many places left that have to cope with good old-fashioned manual labour. Because of the cost of employing stage crews a set may be more simple and stylized, suggesting outlines of buildings, walls, and indoor and outdoor areas. This usually means small cut-away flattage or maybe just pieces of furniture to state where the location is meant to be. Whatever the design the scene change should be worked out early on.

As rehearsals progress, the DSM will keep the stage manager informed of the director's ideas on how he wants to move the characters from scene to scene. The DSM will also make a list of where all the props and furniture are set and where they finish up at the end of a sequence for each scene. The designer will discuss the various items they do not want to use consecutively through the piece. This will tell a stage manager what can be left on and perhaps moved to another part of the set, and the items that have to be struck altogether. Once they have collected as much information from seeing the rehearsals themselves and received notes from the DSM,

the stage manager will sit down with the designer, director, and production manager to discuss how the changes will work. Will they need extra crew or flymen or will the stage management be able to do the changes? Can some of the pieces be made light enough to be handled by one person? Will one flyman be enough or will there be a lot of cross-flying? Cross-flying means one piece going out as another is seen to come in. How many actors are on stage when the change happens or is about to happen? How much is struck and set or used again? How good is access to off-stage left and right or up centre? How much space is there in the wings once off? Can you turn the truck or piece of furniture ready for its re-entrance in another scene or act? Is there somewhere to put the tray or box of struck props, preferably not on top of the items to come on in the newly set scene?

Find a clear route for each team member to prevent them bumping into each other. Take into account any varying levels, as going up and down a staircase or set of treads both on-stage and off with an armful of props is no easy task,

Good Scene-Change Practice

- Everyone should be dressed in uniform black outfits covering them from neck to toe including wrists. In some cases a black balaclava cap (with a face mask, as a terrorist might wear!) and black gloves need to be worn.
- No items should be hanging from a waist belt such as torches, mobile phones or tools.
- Belts should not have large shiny metallic buckles or studs.
- No one should wear glittery jewellery.
- Shoes should not have light-coloured or white soles.
- No one should carry clipboards with their lists attached, there is no time to look at them and it makes carrying props difficult.

- No one should carry lists in back pockets of trousers; remember you are seen as shadows scurrying around the set, it draws unnecessary attention to the individual.
- All SM and Crew must keep to their allocated job and take the same rehearsed route on every scene change.
- Speed and silence are the thing, do not run but be purposeful and brisk.
- Do not talk while setting items.
- Be light of foot and try not to fall over or kick anything.
- Closing your eyes just before entering a darkened set can help you see your way around much more quickly and easily.

Scene-change rehearsal, sorting out how to change from one scene to the next. From the top photograph at the end of one scene to the changed stage in the bottom photograph.

Discussing the best moves. Despite planning scene changes in advance, it is not until you reach the stage and put these plans into action that you see how well they work.
Photos: Rebecca Gibbs

(Right) *Sometimes a member of the company will clear the stage and do the scene change as part of the action.*

(Left) Dead body mark-out in an Agatha Christie thriller. This black body outline had to be laid down quickly during the scene change.

especially quietly and speedily. Even if a piece of scenery or furniture appears light enough for one to carry, it is often quicker and quieter with two doing it, and will look a lot tidier.

Speed, silence and accuracy also apply when setting behind tabs or a cloth. You can be easily heard, as there is not much protection from a set of drapes.

All positions of furniture trucks and pieces of scenery are marked with different-coloured plastic lx tape. These marks need to be small and as few as possible, for when the stage is bare the coloured marks are very distracting. Some designers and directors ask for them to be removed. Always line up with another item on the set or the proscenium arch or maybe a painted pattern on the stage. Only use luminous tape out of necessity, otherwise when the

PAGES **108–111**
A comprehensive, well-written running list ensuring that everything will be done each night in the same organized manner.

107

'THE SNOWMAIDEN'

Running List - Stage Manager (Sarah Morgan)

Pre show:

−50mins   Shout check with ASMs (Gemma Tonge or Laura Streather)

Prologue Beginners:	Onstage	Miss Maria Nikoloulea (US or SR Flipper)
		Miss Isabel Clegg (US of SR Flipper)
		Miss Cinzia Barbotti (US of SR Flipper)
		Mr Luke Baio (US of SR Flipper)
		Mr Adrian Dwyer (DS of SR Flipper)
	SR	Miss Joana Cunha
	SL	Miss Estelle Kaique

Prologue Beginners   Receive SL clearance from Gemma Tonge
Receive SR clearance from Laura Streather
Give Stage clearance to Megan Phillips

Prologue:

Page	Time	Area	Action
13	9mins	Off UR, US of door	On UR cue light, page UR door open for Bird's exit, then close.
20	12mins	Off DR. On sound control underneath working light control panel	Turn volume control for 'Mic' to full for offstage female chorus - Song and Dance of the birds.
		As above	Turn volume control for 'Mic' to off after the Song and Dance of the birds.
67	30mins	Off UR. US of UR door	Cross US of flats with Snowmaiden after she exits UR and clear a path through chorus to the cart. Help into cart. Fetch cup of water from under cart and give to her.
95	40mins	Off UR	Collect cloth from SR prop shelves.
102	42mins	Off DR	Watch gauze in.
		PROLOGUE/ACT 1 CHANGE	

		DC	After chorus have exited, enter UL and mop water from stage. Exit UR and close UR door.
ACT 1			
107	43mins	Off DR	Watch gauze out.
	1hr 12	Off DR	Watch gauze in.

Receive Iron clearance from Megan Phillips that Laura Streather and Gemma Tonge are in position DS of iron.
Give member of on duty staff, and LX, the cue to bring in the iron.

Interval 1 Checklist

Remove snow from dome and place in carrier bag.
Set flower arrangement 1 in the centre of the dome.
Sweep and hoover stage.
Set bed USC
Drop bolts in US holes.
Set Tsar's wheelchair UR on marks.
Set wash basin in it wash cloth on DR corner of bed.
UR & UL doors open.
Other doors shut.

Act 2 Beginners: Ful male voice chorus (14 people)
                      Mr Breffni Horgan/Mr Andrew Rees

On Act 2 Beginners: Assist Mr Horgan/Rees in to bed.
                      Remove slippers from Mr Horgan/Rees
                      Set slippers US of wheelchair
                      Set Male Chorus US of gauze
                      Bring in Blinder
                      Bring in Birdie Bar
                      Mark Newell to check focus of Birdies

Give LX operator clearance when focus check complete
Receive SL clearance from Gemma Tonge
Receive SR clearance from Laura Streather
Give male chorus vocal standby
Give Megan Phillips Stage clearance over cans
Give on-duty member of staff the 'go' for the iron on DR cue light

ACT 2			
	2mins	Off UR. US of door	When male chorus are clear of the stage, receive clearance from Laura Streather and stabilize UR cue light.
	3mins		Shut UR door after Bermyata has entered.
	13mins	Off USC	Lift bolts on bed and strike to dock bay remaining hidden.
	32mins	Off DR	Watch gauze in.
		ACT 2/ACT 3 CHANGE	
ACT 3	F/O	Off UR, US of door	Open UR door to brown marks and set it there.
250	35mins	Off UR. US of door	When chorus standing by for round dance, stabilize UR cue light.
295	50mins	Off UL. US of door	Close door UL after chorus exit.
F/O	F/O	Off RC	FILL BATH WITH WARM WATER FROM PROPS DEPARTMENT.
	1hr8	Off DR	Watch gauze in.

Receive clearance from Megan Phillips that Laura Streather and Gemma Tonge are FOH ready to watch the iron in.
Give member of on-duty staff, and LX, the 'GO' from the iron to come in.

Interval 2 Checklist:

Sweep and hoover DS
Set flower arrangements 2 and 3 in dome, UL and UR of central arrangement
Set the 3 special flowers in dome
SR flipper to perpendicular position
Bath onto yellow marks – check water still warm
Fill the water jugs with warm water
Check there are 3 nails in bath pelmet.

Act 4 Beginners:

Miss Estelle Kaique (onstage in bath)
Miss Sarah Redgwick / Miss Natasha Jouhl (onstage sat at table)
Miss Cinzia Barbotti (off R)
Miss Joana Cunha (off R)
Miss Isabel Clegg (off R)
Miss Maria Nikoloulea (off R)

On beginners:
Receive SR clearance from Laura Streather
Receive SL clearance from Gemma Tonge
Give Megan Phillips stage clearance
On FOH clearance:
Signal to Gemma to leave the stage with Beautiful Spring's dressing gown
Give member of staff, and LX, the go for the iron
Stabilize DR cue light when Gemma is clear of the stage.

ACT 4			
342	0min	Off RC	Remain between DR and RC door after stabilizing cue light.
347	4mins	Off RC	Receive white bath sheet from Miss Cunha.
F/O	F/O	Off RC	Assist Miss Clegg and Miss Nikoloulea to strike bath.
354	9mins	Off RC	Open DR door as flat closes and guide armchair into place.
401		Off UR. US of door	Close UR door on UR cue light.
423	30mins	Off UC	Supervise Mizguir jump.

lights are out the stage tends to look like an airport runway! Luminous tape does not shine backstage unless you have a bright light shining on to it for some while before the area goes dark. White tape and white paint used backstage for safety reasons work well.

When marking furniture and chairs with the coloured plastic tape, use one new colour for each piece of furniture in a new scene and act. For instance Act I Scene i all settings to be marked in blue tape, Act I Scene ii everything marked in red tape, Act II Scene i in yellow tape, and so on. This information would be noted on the scene change list and running list.

Only mark the back legs or US side of a piece of furniture, not all four legs or corners as this makes for too many marks. For circular tables, pouffes, and so on, one small cross for the item to sit on would be sufficient, not small curves or complete circles.

A stage manager will end up with a detailed and efficient scene-change list that has been developing throughout the rehearsal period. They will have concentrated on working out the best route to take items on and off stage, making sure that a table is not carried off with a meal still set on it, or with cutlery, cruet sets or wine glasses still full of liquid. This is so precarious especially when exiting from the stage through a small doorway into equally small and darkened wings. In some circumstances, items may be stuck to a tray or table.

There needs to be fluidity, everyone should be organized to come onto stage with something to set and exit with an item no longer required. There is nothing worse than people wandering on and off stage without seemingly doing anything. There must be a well organized system, that must never vary once it has been rehearsed and found to work.

111

'The Snowmaiden'

Flies Running Plot

Preset

Gauze at IN dead (bar 2)
Birdie bar at OUT dead (bar 3)
Blinder at OUT dead (bar 8)
Moon at Middle IN dead (hemp line)
Sun at farthest OUT dead (bar 39) - at Act 1 out dead i.e. grided
Snow bag full and set (bars 27 & 28)
Border at Act 1 IN dead (bar 37)

Prologue

Page	Time	Q No.	Bar	Description	Action	Speed	Operator
p.2	1min	FLY1	27	SNOW BAG	Snow fall to start	Med	Simon Deacon
p.4	3mins	FLY2	27	SNOW BAG	Snow fall intensifies	Fast	Simon Deacon
p.5	3mins	FLY3	2	GAUZE	To OUT Dead	Med	Louise Rogers
	8mins	FLY 5.1	27	SNOW BAG	Snow fall to finish		Simon Deacon
p.35	14mins	FLY 5.2	27	SNOW BAG	Snow fall to start	Med	Louise Rogers
p.36	14mins	FLY 5.5	27	SNOW BAG	Snow fall to finish		Louise Rogers
	38mins	FLY6	2	GAUZE	To IN Dead	Fast	Louise Rogers
	39mins	F/O	h/f	MOON	To OUT Dead		Louise Rogers
	Sc.CH	FLY7	2	GAUZE	To OUT Dead		Louise Rogers

Act 1

Page	Time	Q No.	Bar	Description	Action	Speed	Operator
p. 178	1h09	FLY8	2	GAUZE	To IN Dead	Fast	Louise Rogers
p. 180	Intervl	FLY 8.5	8	BLINDER	To IN Dead		Louise Rogers
	Intervl	FLY 8.7	3	BIRDIE	To IN Dead		Louise Rogers
	Intervl	F/O	2	GAUZE	OUT slightly to allow access to dome		Louise Rogers
	Intervl	F/O	2	GAUZE	To IN Dead		Louise Rogers

A well-written fly plot giving full details of the flying for the show. A strange operator could fly the show easily with this documentation.

Act 2

Page	Time	Q No.	Bar	Description	Action	Speed	Operator
p. 190	4mins	FLY 9	8	BLINDER	To OUT Dead	Fast	Simon Deacon
p. 190	4mins	FLY 9.5	3	BIRDIE	To OUT dead	Fast	Louise Rogers
p. 190	4mins	FLY 10	2	GAUZE	To OUT dead	Med	Louise Rogers
p. 250	32mins	FLY 11	2	GAUZE	To IN dead	Fast	Louise Rogers
	Sc.Ch	FLY 11.5	h/f	MOON	To middle IN Dead		Louise Rogers

Act 3

Page	Time	Q No.	Bar	Description	Action	Speed	Operator
p. 255	36min	FLY 12	2	GAUZE	To OUT Dead	Med	Louise Rogers
p. 336	1h03	FLY 13	2	GAUZE	To IN dead	Fast	Louise Rogers
	Intervl	F/O	39	SUN	To IN Dead		Louise Rogers
	Intervl	F/O	37	BORDER	To Act 4 OUT dead		Louise Rogers
	Intervl	F/O	2	GAUZE	OUT slightly to allow access to dome		Louise Rogers
	Intervl	F/O	2	GAUZE	To IN Dead		Louise Rogers

Act 4

Page	Time	Q No.	Bar	Description	Action	Speed	Operator
341	3mins	FLY 14	2	GAUZE	To OUT Dead	Med	Louise Rogers
	15mins	FLY 14.5	h/f	MOON	To Act 4 IN Dead	V. Slow over 2 mins	Louise Rogers
398		FLY 15	39	SUN	To 1st OUT Dead (to be complete by Misguir's exit over flat) then to 2nd Out Dead by end of Opera	Med until top of sun appears then v.v.slow	Louise Rogers
After Calls		FLY 16	2	GAUZE	To IN Dead		Louise Rogers

NOTE:

On Stage: Yellow/Green marks for doors are for opening doors parallel to the front of the stage.

Brown marks for doors are for opening doors perpendicular to the flats. (Only used for cart exits.)

In Flies: In Dead = Yellow/Green

Out Dead = Blue

All other variations are marked on the fly ropes.

9 REHEARSAL ROOMS

WHAT TO LOOK FOR

The ideal rehearsal room simply does not exist. There are so many facilities on a stage manager's wish list that the rehearsal room would have to be purpose-built. Some companies are lucky enough to operate in theatres that have a rehearsal room within the building. This is a considerable luxury and even these have their drawbacks as they are often at the very top of the building or in the basement where there is no natural light.

To a certain extent the rehearsal room you need depends upon the type of production you are rehearsing. A large company who are rehearsing a musical will require a room that can accommodate perhaps fifty people or more, a piano, is mirrored down one long side and is big enough to contain all the props for a 20-scene epic. If you are rehearsing a two-hander, that is a play with only two characters in it, which is emotionally draining and very intimate, you may find that a darkened basement room out of the way of the general bustle is the ideal place to rehearse.

In practice you generally have very little choice. In the major cities, especially London, there is usually a range of rehearsal rooms to choose from. In the provinces and especially when working for a regional rep you will probably have only two different church or community halls to choose from.

London rehearsal rooms are varied, fairly plentiful and very expensive. They are listed in a directory called *Contacts* that is published by Spotlight and is renewed annually. It contains many useful contact names and telephone numbers from props suppliers to agents' contact numbers. Many of the London rehearsal rooms are as close as you get to the ideal and some have been built or adapted specifically to hire out to television and theatre companies as rehearsal rooms. These rooms are large, usually have natural light, are available for exclusive use and come with extra facilities such as a stage manager's office and telephone. They often include a kitchen and sometimes a smaller room adjacent to the main rehearsal space. Consequently they are very expensive and difficult to book as television companies usually hire them for a long period of time.

In smaller cities where the choices are limited and your productions have an average cast of ten actors there are other basic practicalities, which need to be considered. Providing the hall is large enough to allow for a mark-up of the main acting area of your stage, the next thing to consider is how convenient the rest of the facilities are.

The distance from the rehearsal room to your base theatre is very important. Remember that apart from the actual rehearsals all the other work for the production will be carried out in the theatre, all wardrobe fittings, prop finding, lighting plans and sound recording will, with the occasional exception, be carried out back at the theatre. One of the essential elements for a successful production is good communication between all departments and if this is hampered by too great a distance between rehearsals and the staging departments it will make your life as a stage manager much more difficult. You should be present at the beginning of rehearsals each day and at the end. There will be countless other visits to the rehearsal and a lot of time is lost sitting in the van travelling between the rehearsal room and your theatre.

Natural light is always high on the list of requirements especially as far as the director is concerned. It is very tiring rehearsing for hours each day under fluorescent light or poor light. Directors will sometimes request additional lighting from the theatre to be rigged in the rehearsal room if the existing lighting is poor. This creates quite a lot of extra work even if it is possible. The electricity supply of some halls is not powerful enough to safely run theatre lighting from it even if the chief electrician can spare the equipment.

If the hall does have natural light check that it can be blacked out. Is there sufficient curtaining to shade the actors from a dazzling sunset shining right into their eyes as they rehearse? Can the director create a semi-dark room at midday, if necessary?

Given that many acting companies are closeted in a rehearsal room every day for a minimum of three weeks it is worth checking for facilities that will make life easier throughout this period. The rehearsal room should be large enough to allow actors to sit around the room when they are not actually rehearsing or are waiting to make their entrance. Ideally there will be another small room available where they can read, learn their lines or rehearse a short scene with another actor away from the main rehearsal. This additional room can be very useful for a number of other reasons such as wardrobe fittings if the hall and the theatre are close enough for the wardrobe staff to visit rehearsals. Press and radio interviews can be carried out in this room without disturbing the main rehearsal, even photographs can be taken here. If an actor has to leave the rehearsal room and go elsewhere for any of these things much of their time is wasted going to and fro.

Another useful additional facility is a kitchen or small area away from the main rehearsal where tea and coffee can be made. Tea and coffee or an alternative should always be available and it is much easier to contain the inevitable mess and clear up afterwards if there is a kitchen. A kitchen is also useful for preparing any rehearsal food that may be required and for the company to use at lunchtime, particularly if it has a microwave.

Most church and community halls have kitchens attached but the use of these facilities is not always included in the basic hire charge.

Access to a telephone is also important, many people now have mobile phones but these should be turned off in the rehearsal room. The DSM may have their mobile phone on mute or vibrate in rehearsals in order that they can be contacted. A better arrangement is a telephone within earshot of the rehearsals but not actually in the room itself. Stage management will need to make and receive calls during rehearsals but there are many times when this is better done in private. A crucial responsibility for the ASM in rehearsals is answering the telephone and relaying any messages accurately and quickly to the DSM.

Getting to the rehearsal room and once there getting into the actual room is also an important consideration. There will be a number of people attending rehearsals all at different times and it is important that they can reach the venue easily either by public or private transport and once there, gain access to the building when required. A rehearsal room that is difficult to get to on public transport, has no parking nearby and needs a security code to get in is not worth the hassle. As well as access for people, stage management will need to bring rehearsal props and furniture into the room. Leaving a van outside on double yellow lines whilst you and your team struggle up three flights of stairs with a rehearsal sofa does not make a good start to the day. Ideally the rehearsal room will have its own parking, be on ground level and have double access doors directly into a spacious, light, warm, soundproofed hall with its own kitchen and telephone. Unfortunately there are very few rehearsal rooms that fit all these criteria.

WHERE TO LOOK

Many regional theatres have a rehearsal room that they have used for many years, but if for some reason this is no longer possible or you go to work in a theatre without a regular rehearsal room you will need to look for a new one.

Church and community halls will be the sort of hall you will be looking for and a good place to start is under this category in your local yellow pages or business directory. Entries under halls, churches and community centres all provide a list from which to work. A telephone call will eliminate those that are too far away, too expensive or not available during the day. Sometimes it is useful to get in a car and drive round the area close to the theatre. Many halls have a notice outside giving the name of the hall and the name and telephone number of the caretaker. This will also give you an opportunity to view the property at least from the outside. You can then eliminate any halls that are inaccessible, probably too small or difficult to find.

CHECKING SPACE AND FACILITIES

Once you have decided to look at a particular hall in more detail you will want to establish from the caretaker what facilities the hall has. If the hall does have facilities such as a kitchen, telephone, and additional small room it is worth checking these out in great detail.

You must check that the hire fee includes the use of the kitchen or if not how much more you will have to pay. Sometimes you are allowed access to the kitchen but all the cupboards and drawers are locked because the cutlery and crockery belong to the Mothers' Union. If you are allowed to use the equipment you will have to pay for any breakages, and be meticulous in cleaning the kitchen at the end of the day. Likewise, if there is an additional room, is this included in the hire charge, would you have exclusive use of the room and is it accessible at the same time as the main rehearsal room? Do you need a separate key for it, for example? As far as a telephone is concerned, occasionally the hall will operate a sort of meter system whereby you are able to use the telephone as if it was a private line and the cost of the calls is added to your weekly bill. This system is usually only found in established London rehearsal rooms. The alternative is invariably a pay phone; this may be a card phone or one that takes coins. This will be paid for from petty cash and is another cost that stage management cannot know in advance but for which they have to budget before they bring their final costings to the first production meeting.

It is very important to visit a new hall before you make a booking to use it. However suitable it may seem when described by the caretaker, only you as the stage manager can decide how good it will be as a rehearsal space. For example the floor area may be very large in terms of square metres but on inspection the pillars, arches or overhangs that protrude into the space may make any useful mark-up impossible. You cannot expect a caretaker to understand these limitations.

During your visit you should also take careful note of the amount of storage space in the hall.

Where Is the Door?

It is worth marking up the set so that the door to the rehearsal room is on the DSM's left or right. It is very distracting if someone entering the room has to walk across the mark-up to reach the DSM or director. Once inside the room you should be able to reach the DSM by the shortest, most unobtrusive route possible.

It is surprising how much storage space you will need once the hall is full of rehearsal props and furniture. It is often the case that you will be sharing the room with evening activities such as the bridge club and you will need to pack everything away at the end of the day. Even if the evening activities can happen around your rehearsal props and furniture you need to lock them all away each evening to be sure that they are all there the next morning. It has been known for an enthusiastic cleaner to remove half the props thinking that they were rubbish. They may have looked like actual rubbish to most people but to the stage management team they represented a long props list. Adequate storage space on the premise will save a lot of time that would otherwise be spent loading a van and returning all the props and furniture to the theatre each night and back again the following morning. Use of the hall can become a major issue. You need to make it very clear if you will require the hall in the evenings and on Saturdays. The theatrical week means six days, Monday to Saturday inclusive from 9:00am to 10:00pm or later. The caretaker will assume a week to mean Monday to Friday inclusive from 9:00am to 5:00pm. These discrepancies can have serious consequences for the rehearsal schedule if they are not cleared up when you book the hall. Any booking must be agreed in writing and days, dates and times meticulously recorded and confirmed.

It is also worth taking note of the condition of the floor and walls when visiting the hall. A beautifully polished floor and newly decorated walls will ring alarm bells for an experienced stage manager. The ideal tape to use for a mark-up, that is, coloured pvc sticky tape, will cause havoc on a polished floor, leaving a sticky residue on the surface and a large bill in your in-tray. Alternatively, a floor in a very poor condition will not be easy to mark out on and runs the risk of splinters for the company and a very dusty rehearsal period. There are alternatives to the pvc tape such as cotton tape and chalk but these are not as convenient as pvc. Avoiding damage to newly decorated walls is easier, you can provide a free-standing notice-board for the company to use but there is still a risk that an enthusiastic actor will stick a piece of research on the wall with self-adhesive tape. It is possible to overcome most of these problems; the important thing is to talk to the caretaker making sure that they understand the peculiar requirements of a rehearsal. You must make sure that anything that you regard as normal will not upset your relationship with the hall owners and likewise that none of their restrictions will prevent your company from rehearsing the play fully. For example the Catholic Church may take offence if their hall is used to rehearse a play that criticizes the Pope, some caretakers require stage management to remove the mark-up at the end of each day because the floor needs to be smooth for a ballet class.

Finally two small but crucial points to clarify before booking a hall: who will be responsible for cleaning it and how will you gain entry each day? If you are responsible for cleaning, will you have access to suitable equipment such as brooms and a vacuum cleaner? If you are not responsible, will you have to pay a deposit in advance to cover the cost of cleaning or will there be a bill to come after the rehearsal period has finished? Getting into the hall easily each day is obviously very important. Caretakers are reluctant to hand over keys for an entire rehearsal period unless you have hired the hall on a regular basis and there have been no problems in the past. This is the best arrangement, but if you are not allowed to keep a key you must make it very clear when you will require access. Remember to allow time for your team to set up before rehearsals start and to clear away afterwards. The last problem you want at the start of the day is the company waiting on the doorstep and no sign of the caretaker with the magic key.

10 THE PRODUCTION WEEK

THE GET-IN

Once the strike of the previous show is complete, the get-in for the already built pieces of the next production's set begins.

The stage management on this day will be extremely busy. There will be rehearsals taking place in an outside rehearsal room, or if you are lucky there may be an upstairs bar area or large dressing room in your theatre where the company can work.

The production manager would have organized the strike and get-out of the previous show into the get-in and fit-up of the new production. The schedule of work would be set out as illustrated on pages 119–120.

Before anyone is able to work on-stage the stage needs to be clear and well swept. A chalked mark-out of the set would be put down on the stage. Possibly the floor would need to be painted, maybe there would be already painted floorboards or a stage cloth to be laid. This work could take several hours, and it would have been worked out by the production manager and all heads of department before the schedule is decided. If the floor is white or of a similar delicate colour or maybe the material used is easily marked or scuffed, a later time in the schedule would be planned to deal with the floor laying and/or painting, when most of the heavy work on stage had been completed.

Stage Management Duties Leading up to the Technical Rehearsal

These jobs do vary with the size of the production. The following is for an average-sized show, and a team of four stage management, the SM, DSM, two ASMs.

The SM and one ASM on stage assisting in the fit-up, at the same time dealing with possible publicity or photo calls and organizing final costume fittings.

The DSM making sure the company and director are being serviced. (They may start the rehearsals off and return to the stage to assist in the fit-up.)

The second ASM would be returning props from the previous show and collecting last-minute items including any hired props and furniture and perishable supplies needed for the new production.

Once the lighting is in progress, the SM would be around setting up prop tables and organizing the wing space. They are available if needed by the lighting designer.

The DSM would be at the production desk with the script, marking in the lighting cues.

The ASMs would alternate between walking for lights and helping the SM to set up the wings, and possibly finishing off small props, such as putting sealing wax on scrolls or letters and sticking leaves onto a branch, etc.

'CABARET'

<u>Production Schedule</u>

Sat, 11th Nov	NIGHT	GET OUT Fashion, FIT UP Cabaret
Sun, 12th Nov	AM	Continue fit up
	13.00–14.00	BREAK
	14.00–18.00	Continue fit up
	18.00–19.00	BREAK
	19.00–23.00	FOCUS
Mon, 13th Nov	09.00–13.00	FOCUS
	(10.00–13.00	Band call. Short Street)
	13.00–14.00	BREAK
	14.00–18.00	FOCUS
	(14.00–17.00	Band call. Short Street)
	18.00–19.00	BREAK
	19.00–23.00	LIGHT
	(18.00–21.00	Band call. Short Street)
Tues, 14th Nov	09.00–13.00	LIGHT
	(10.00–13.00	Band call with Company. Short St.)
	13.00–14.00	BREAK
	14.00–14.30	Company into costume
	14.30–18.00	TECH ACT I
	18.00–19.00	BREAK
	19.00–23.00	TECH ACT I
Wed, 15 Nov	09.00 13.00	LIGHT
	(10.00–13.00	Band call with Company. Short St)
	13.00–14.00	BREAK
	14.00–14.30	Company into costume
	14.00–18.00	TECH ACT II
	18.00–19.00	BREAK
	19.00–23.00	TECH ACT 11
Thurs, 16th Nov	09.00–10.00	Set up Band area
	10.00–13.00	Band set up and sound balance
	13.00–14.00	BREAK
	14.00–18.00	Continue sound balance with Co.
	18.00–19.00	BREAK
	19.00–19.30	Company into costume
	19.30–23.00	Dress rehearsal (PRODUCTION PHOTOS)
Fri, 17th Nov	09.00–12.45	Free for tech work on set
	12.45–13.45	BREAK
	13.15	Company into costume
	13.45	Press Photo call
	14.00–18.00	Dress rehearsal
	18.00–19.25	BREAK
	20.00	First Preview Performance

Production schedule for a performance of **Cabaret,** *including band calls.*

'M. BUTTERFLY'

Third Draft Schedule

Sun 19 March	NIGHT	Fit up M. BUTTERFLY
Mon 20 March	09.00–13.00	Continue Fit up
	14.00–18.00	LX Focus - Musicians seated
	19.00–23.00	LX Focus
	23.00–03.00	Lighting plot?
Tues 21 March	09.00–13.00	Sound balance with musicians
	13.00–14.00	BREAK
	14.00–18.00	Light with J.D. - word run for Co. in rehearsal room
	18.00–19.00	BREAK
	19.00–23.00	Start Tech rehearsal - Korogo + Jamie and Michelle
	23.00	Paint call
Wed 22 March	09.00–13.00	Lighting with J.D.
	13.00–14.00	BREAK
	14.00–18.00	Tech rehearsal
	18.00–19.00	BREAK
	19.00–23.00	Tech rehearsal
Thurs 23 March	09.00–13.00	Tech work on set
	13.00–14.00	BREAK
	14.00–18.00	Tech rehearsal
	18.00–19.00	BREAK
	19.00–23.00	Tech rehearsal
Fri 24 March	09.00–13.00	Tech work on set
	13.00–14.00	BREAK
	14.00–18.00	Dress rehearsal
	18.00–19.00	BREAK
	19.00	Dress rehearsal
Sat 25 March	09.00–13.00	Lighting adjustment
	13.00–14.00	BREAK
	14.00–18.00	Rehearsal as called
	20.00	First Preview

Production schedule for **Madame Butterfly**. *Note this is the third draft. It is always difficult to fit everyone in, hence this third attempt.*

The production manager together with his master carpenter and assistant plus a casual crew person and the stage management, would bring all the flats and sections of the set from the workshop to the stage. Then they put them in order of how they will be erected on the

relevant sides of the stage. Usually all the pieces are marked as to whether they are for stage right or left.

Usually working from the downstage to the upstage bars, flying pieces are laid out on stage one bar at a time, the bars are dropped in, the item is attached, then flown out. Sometimes the flown pieces will need battening together before being flown, or hanging irons screwed to the bottom of the flat to help take the weight of the piece from the bottom rather than allowing undue stress at the top of the flat. While the work on stage is happening the electrics department will be rigging front of house (front of house is the area of the auditorium which does not include the stage). Once the flats start being erected it will have been agreed within the schedule that rigging will work around the build.

As the fit-up nears its completion and the Lx are about to focus all the rigged lanterns, the stage management in conjunction with the designer and director start to mark the furniture positions, which is necessary for the focusing. The marks would be the measured marks from your ground plan that you have noted down before leaving the rehearsal room after the final run-through.

(Above) A flyman's view of a bar flying in.

Battening out a flying piece before attaching it to the bar and flying it out.

BAR NO.	Distance From wall (m)	PENTECOST			
		ITEM	Kg	Weights	Notes
		1 weight = 12.25kg (28lbs)			
CYC	10.25	Surround Blacks (tracked)			
40	SR side bar	Border			
39	8.8	Border/legs			
38	SL side bar				
37	8.47				
36	8.28				
35	8.09				
34	7.88	Lx bar 5			
33	7.66				
32	7.49				
31	7.33	Legs			
30	7.1	Border			
29	6.73				
28	6.53	Lx Bar 4			
27	6.33				
26	6.13				
25	5.94				
24	5.55	Legs			
23	5.35	Border			
22	5.14				
21	4.95				
20	4.76				
19	4.57	Legs			
18	4.37	Border			
17	4.17				
16	3.97				
15	3.78				
14	3.59	Lx Bar 3			
13	3.2	Legs			
12	2.99	Border			
11	2.79				
10	2.59				
09	2.39	Cloth			
08	2.2	Calico Flat			
07	1.98	Brick Flat			
06	1.78	Border			
05	1.58				
Winch	1.52	Lx Bar 2			
04	1.38				
03	1.1				
02	0.91	Lx Bar 1			
01	0.62				
Total Weight					

A hanging plot showing on which bars pieces of masking, lighting and scenery will be hung. The number of counterweights for each piece are also recorded.

Hanging a flown flat.

Useful Equipment

Blue tack
Staple gun and staples
Copydex
Super glue
Velcro self-sticking tape
Double-sided tape
Small torch

The director will return to his rehearsal and you and the designer will continue to dress the set. Some of the dressing could be dealt with while the focus session is in progress, this means setting items and often sticking them down while in the dark, as the lanterns are being set (focused) to shine on specific areas or pieces of furniture with all other lights out. There will never be the ideal situation when you would have working light or time to yourself on stage for dressing the set or setting props.

The stage manager should give all the practicals, such as table lamps, standard lamps, ceiling lights and anything else that plugs into an electrical socket, to the electrics department, so they are able to wire up the various appliances.

Once the focus has been completed, the lighting session begins. The lighting designer collates all the rigged and focused lanterns. When they are brought up by the board operator there is overall light onto the various stage areas – this becomes a lighting state. He will then proceed to plot different states into the board with the board operator, each state will become a cue, and the director and set designer in conjunction with the lighting designer will plot where these cues will be placed in the script.

The DSM who will be sitting with the creative team at the production desk, will be told by the director and lighting designer where to mark the cue points in the script. This is also when the DSM will put in the standbys for these cues. An ASM will walk the set as instructed by the director and lighting designer. This is done to give the creative team an idea of what the actors will look like in the various lighting states.

Walking for Lights

- When walking for lighting you should wear dark clothes unless you have been asked for a white shirt for a specific costume effect.
- Do not wear a hat or cap unless asked; it may be important to see how very fair hair or very dark hair look under the lights. Most importantly the designer and director must be able to see your face.
- Walk slowly across the stage when asked to walk from point A to point B. This action enables the designer to see black spots or areas that need a re-focus or extra lantern.

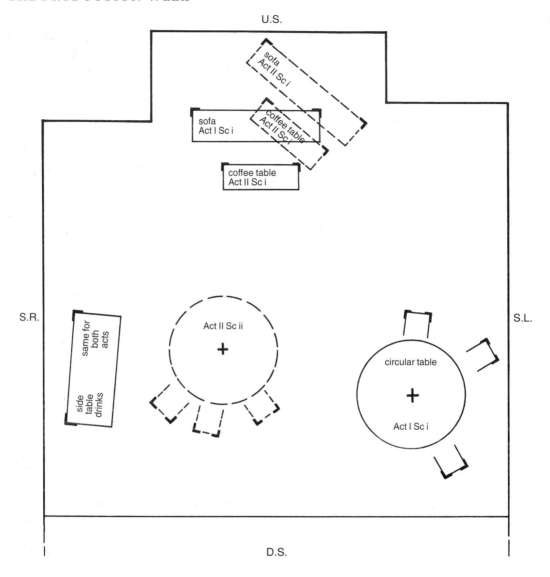

How to mark furniture – the bold marks show which edges should be marked by placing tape in the corresponding position on the stage floor.

The SM and second ASM will not be far away in case the set needs changing as the creative team light through the play. It also gives the SM and their assistant time to set the props onto the already prepared tables off-stage. The stage manager is able to catch up on updating some of the lists and paperwork for the notice-board, preparing the name cards for the dressing room doors, completing any last-minute prop jobs such as sticking and sewing, sealing wax on scrolls or letters, making up parcels.

The sound department will have rigged and tested around the fit-up and the electrics rig. There will also be a scheduled time of silence arranged for the operator to have a sound session with the director, where levels would be decided and perhaps the length of some of the cues, such as birds, wind and music.

TECHNICAL REHEARSALS

At the half-hour call on the day of the technical rehearsal the stage manager would possibly be urging various technicians off the stage as they try and complete last-minute jobs – for instance, calling to an ASM for the dustpan and brush to sweep up the wood shavings and old nails and screws, as the workshop tried to make the door open and close properly.

With your stage management team you would have organized the wing space and prop tables, quick-change areas for the wardrobe, and the position for the prompt desk making sure the sight lines are as good as can be. In a lot of theatres the prompt desk position is static either backstage or in the control box at the back of the circle or stalls. Sight lines would be marked down on the floor. These are lines which, if anyone steps over them, will be seen by the audience. Obviously an actor wants to be seen but only when it is intended. For reference, tape or pin all the required setting and running lists to the walls and backs of flats, making sure the flats do not move during the action of the play!

The DSM with another member of the team will check the show relay, tannoy system and all cue lights and headsets. The DSM will give all calls from the half hour call over the tannoy. The SM will allocate one of the ASMs to check and set all personal props, they will check that all the company have arrived in their dressing rooms, reporting to their stage manager any unscheduled absentees. If necessary, the stage manager will then phone around to try and find out what has happened to the missing actor.

The stage manager just before the half hour call would organize themselves and an ASM to shout check the props. This means making sure that there is nothing missing and everything is set in the order of scenes and acts, and details, such as the teapot with its spout facing the right way and in the correct position, are checked. Everything that is used gets listed and checked. The stage manager does the calling reading from the setting list and the ASM checks each prop and piece of furniture and those items that are always there that actors get used to using, such as chairs and small tables. It is a good idea to make space in the wings for chairs for the actors to use when they come off-stage and before they re-enter – sometimes there is no time for them to return to the dressing rooms between their scenes and they prefer to remain in the wings. The details of the positions of these chairs must be noted and consistently set each performance. There is a story of a well-known actor who always made an exit off-stage and sat in this chair in the wings close to the prop table. The chair was not a prop or piece of furniture for the show but was a regular chair that had been left in the wings. One night it had been removed, it was very dark, the actor came off-stage, made to sit down in the chair that was not there and fell heavily injuring his back so badly he could not complete the run.

The full company will be called to the stage. The DSM will have arranged for the cast to bring any valuables such as money, purses, wristwatches or pieces of personal jewellery to the prompt desk where they will be locked in a box and kept safe by the DSM until the end of a session when the actors will be able to retrieve their belongings. The cast will then assemble in the stalls where the director will have a talk with them about how they intend the technical rehearsal to run, and specific stops and times will be suggested for certain potentially difficult technical sequences.

The stage manager would then ask the actors to walk the set with them in groups of six if it is a large cast or twos if it is small. The smaller numbers make for better concentration as there is a lot for everyone to take in. The space at each exit and entrance would be pointed out, plus get-offs, and the positions of cue lights reminding them that it is a red light to stand by and a green light to enter or speak if they have lines off-stage. In some theatres the red light flashes and has to be pressed to make it stable. This action will also stabilize the light on the DSM's desk, who will then know the actor or technician is standing by. If it is not a flashing light, then the actor or technician will press the red button to flash the DSM to say they are standing by. The company will also be shown the prop tables and their own specific props. They will also be shown any particular ways to open and close doors or windows.

The stage manager and the DSM should have pre-planned how they will run their side of the technical rehearsal. You must make sure you prevent wasting the valuable time of both the director and the company by poor or no organization of scene changes and technical issues concerning yourself and the team. The stage manager must have all the required paperwork and have handed out the necessary details to each member of the team such as setting lists and running lists, plus a list of beginners that states where the actors are set before the start of the show. They may be set on stage inside a piece of set or cupboard, in the wings or at the back of the auditorium. Each ASM should be allocated to run the stage left wing and stage right wing. If the stage manager has not had time to rehearse the scene changes before this point, this would be the time to talk through the details with the team, explaining the allocated lists and reading with them their duties for each change. This helps them all to understand what happens, and they feel more familiar with the event when it is reached.

The stage manager would ask the director if there were any particular tricky sequences in

Act One that they would need to rehearse before the technical rehearsal starts. This may be a fight scene with blood bags, or gunshots, or smashing a bottle over someone's head.

With the props and stage checked, the walking of the set with the actors completed, and after the director has had his talk with the actors, there will follow a pleasant but authoritative call from the SM requesting that everyone clear the stage and take their positions to start the show from the top of Act One. The DSM also organizes all those operators in the technical areas who would be on headsets to be ready to start the technical rehearsal. Switching on their red cue lights the DSM will ask each area in turn to stand by, only asking the next operator on their list when the previous person had acknowledged both verbally and by cue light. In this way the DSM knows that everyone is ready and there are no problems.

The conversation would be read out as it was written in the prompt copy:

DSM:	Stand by	
Lx Qs 1 2 3 4 5 & 6		(before the next set of cues the Lx Operator would acknowledge the cue light and say: Standing by for Lx Qs 1 2 3 4 5 and 6)
Snd Qs 1 2 and 3		(The Sound Operator would answer as the Lx above)
Fly Q 1		(The Flyman would answer as above)

While the DSM is dealing with the standbys, the stage manager will be organizing the stage moving the cast into their beginning positions with crew and ASMs standing by for their first action of the show. Checking that the working lights are all out and the pre-set is up, you would then call to the DSM that you were all standing by and that they had clearance, which means they are clear for their first cue. This verbalizing between

A fight scene ending with a gunshot such as this would certainly be rehearsed slowly, perhaps before the technical started. Photo: Laurence Burns

the SM and DSM without the use of the headsets means that everyone in the auditorium, the company and crew all know that the rehearsal has started, or when it is necessary to stop and set back the scene. The DSM can confirm the best line of text to pick up the scene that works for their cueing. The DSM will not be able to see the stage clearly enough to call for any flown pieces in or out. The flyman must only hear the voice of the stage manager calling from the stage during a technical rehearsal, an interval change or when setting up for a performance. The stage manager must never walk away once they have given the order for a bar to fly in, they must place themselves centre stage in front of the flown piece with their back towards the auditorium. If necessary, someone should watch each end of the bar as it flies in or out, in case the end of the cloth or scenery needs to be guided past head height. The stage manager must also make sure the company are not in the way while this action is happening. They can be sent into the stalls until all is set and ready to restart. Flying bars in and out can be very dangerous in this situation but by following this procedure you help to minimize this risk.

The DSM at any time may call out and tell the SM that they are ready and set back to do the scene again; this enables the SM to smoothly start the scene and not have to wait while everyone asks if everyone else is ready!

The importance of pre-planning this act of clear communication between the SM and DSM as well as the director, cast, teams and crew cannot be emphasized enough. It is a lot easier if the stage manager, DSM and ASMs know their show really well and are able to anticipate some of the settings and cues and have the actors standing by in the correct places with the right props.

The stage manager must let the front of house manager know the running times of the production, how long each act is and where the intervals (if there is more than one) will come.

The DSM must warn the bars and front of house that an interval or final curtain are coming up by giving them one or two bar bells as a warning. These bells need to be marked in your script – check with your bar how many minutes' warning they would prefer. It is usually approximately ten minutes, which gives them time to lay out the bar orders and the ushers to gather their ice cream trays.

Be prepared, technical rehearsals are long and very tiring however efficiently run. Stage management need to be prepared for odd break times and often short ones with little sleep, so make sure you have plenty of sandwiches and biscuits, soft drinks and bottles of water. In the

Tips for a DSM

Have a packet of small sticky-backed notes to jot down cues that get moved. Rather than take up time in the middle of a technical rehearsal, the altered cues can be marked on the note and stuck over the old cue. The special adhesive on the back of these notes allows you to remove them and reuse them without damage to the script.

If you run out of space for writing standbys, extra cues or sometimes blocking at the top of a page, cut a flap of paper and stick it at the top of a cue column.

Have a notebook to jot down notes about cues or any point that should not go directly into the prompt book.

A large soft clean eraser is a vital piece of equipment.

You will need several pencils with finely sharpened points. Always use pencil – never coloured pencils or inks – for notating cues. Sixty per cent of the time cues move during the technical and dress rehearsals, and often during performances. Once the cue point moves the cue number and standby also have to move.

winter make up a thermos of soup – it is always welcome when the last break arrives. An average technical rehearsal usually runs four times longer than its playing time, so with a three hour show it could total twelve hours or more. However, this does depend on the technical complexities of the piece; it could be longer!

COSTUME CALLS, WIG CALLS, REHEARSAL CALLS, BAND CALLS

The last week of rehearsal is a time when all the loose ends are coming together and the individual contributions of all the staging departments are being finalized. Consequently all these departments need various company members for final fittings or last-minute rehearsals of small scenes. If the production is a musical then it is not until the final week that the whole band will be called to rehearse the orchestral music both with and without the acting company. These last-minute calls continue into the production week, as it is not until the first night and sometimes later that all aspects of the production will be finalized. Stage management are still responsible for

issuing these calls and must take even greater care to ensure that none of the different calls clash resulting in an actor being double booked. Many calls will have to be simultaneous and therefore as a stage manager you will be involved in finding additional space, perhaps for the band to rehearse or for the director to go over a particular scene with two actors whilst the rest of the company rehearse on the main stage or are involved in the band call.

It is important that these calls are kept up to date and posted on all notice-boards just as they have been during earlier rehearsals. These calls are over and above the production schedule that gives an overview of the production week and are also subject to change at short notice. As a broad rule the production schedule is primarily concerned with the technical preparations for the show and the stage management are still responsible for calls concerning only the acting company. The production schedule, for instance, would not give details of an extra wardrobe call for two of the company but it will state when the first dress rehearsal is intended to take place. There is a temptation to rely on the production schedule but this must be resisted. You will be extremely busy throughout the

The stage manager Sue Dempsey and choreographer Bill Deamer discuss a changed call during the production week of **Grand Hotel,** *Guildhall School of Music and Drama.*

129

production week but you must make sure that all necessary calls are put up, amended and followed up as accurately as possible.

SETTING UP THE WINGS, PROPS TABLES AND QUICK-CHANGE AREAS

After the first session of the fit up, the bulk of the set will have started to take shape on the stage and this will be sufficient for you to see exactly how much space is available backstage. You will have had an idea from the ground plan but you will now be able to see those useful little spaces where props and furniture can be stored. The positions of any large pieces of scenery or trucks should be planned in advance using a scaled template of the piece and fitting it onto the ground plan. These pieces should be positioned in the wings first but if this is not possible it is important that their position is marked with white tape. This should be done even if they are available as it is useful to have their position in the wings marked when these pieces are on stage. This means that in the scene change they can be returned to the same place. Once these areas have been established it is possible to put the props tables in place. Props tables should be positioned in the most appropriate place and be just large enough to accommodate the props that are set on them. It is much better to have a number of tables dotted around backstage closest to where the props on them are needed rather than two large beautifully laid out tables against the wing wall miles from actors' entrances. Props can be stored on hooks nailed into the back of the set or placed under backstage staircases out of the way of actors' entrances.

Large items such as luggage should never be placed on a table but should be on the floor under or at the end of the table. Smaller items on the table should be placed at the front with taller ones such as vases of flowers at the back. There is much less danger of knocking other

A props table set under a get-off staircase backstage, including props set at the end of the table and large ones on the floor.

props over when reaching for a particular item if the table is laid out in this way. Props that are related to each other, such as all the items required for a tea tray, should be laid out together. In this case the tray would be already set and facing the right way for the actor to pick it up and carry it straight on-stage.

Props tables should also be laid out in specific scenes. The table itself should be covered with a large piece of paper (lining paper or newsprint is ideal) and then sectioned off according to the number of acts and scenes needed to document the props on that table. The props for each scene should be kept together and all the scenes in a particular act would be laid out alongside each other. Depending upon the setting list there may be no props on that particular table for Act One Scene i

Props table laid out, set and checked. Note the space for the two daggers waiting to be set at the last minute.

(Below) An aerial view of a quick-change area stage left during Salisbury Playhouse's pantomime.

(Below right) A quick-change rail set in the wings.

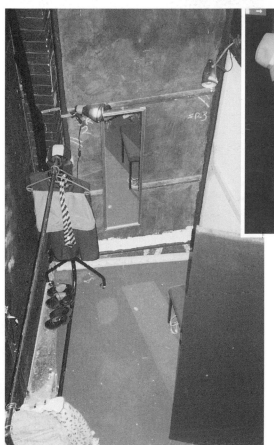

therefore the convention would be followed for the first appropriate act and scene.

Once this has been done it is time to place the actual prop in its appropriate place and then to draw round it. This means that the place for this prop is instantly recognizable when it is returned to the props table and also it is immediately obvious which prop is missing if it is not there during the shout check.

Quick-change areas should also be set up at this time and whilst the production manager as part of the fit up may do this, it is worth checking where it is intended to go. Quick-change areas should be in the wings but there is usually only room for one area each side of the stage. There will not be enough room for one outside every exit or entrance where an actor would like to do a change. Therefore there should be a clear route through the wing from the set to the quick-change area. There should be as much privacy as possible (quick changes have been known to involve a total change including underwear) and this can often be achieved by flattage or drapes hung to form a small room. There should be enough room for a small table and a mirror with a light above it. Usually there will be no door to this area though sometimes it is necessary to have a drape across the entrances similar to those in changing rooms in a clothes shop especially if the light for the mirror could spill onstage. There should also be space to hang costumes and to lay them out

ready for the quick change. After providing all these facilities the quick-change area should be as small as possible, all of the elements may be there but it will still be a bit of a squeeze.

CUE LIGHTS AND HEADSETS

During the final run-throughs in the rehearsal room you and your DSM need to note how many headsets and cue lights you are likely to need. The DSM should note in their book the points where the company may need cue lights for their entrances and you will be aware of cue lights for scene changes. Where these cues appear in the text is the responsibility of the DSM but where the actual light itself will be placed backstage is up to you.

Every theatre has a limited number of headsets and cue lights and they are usually maintained and rigged by the sound department or the

---

Cue Lights for Actors

The DSM will be asked to put many cues in the book for cue lights for the actors' ordinary entrances, most of which will be cut during the technical and dress rehearsals. Generally speaking it is much better for an actor to time himself for his entrance and not to take his cue from the DSM. Many actors need the security of a cue light until they become familiar with the set and the lighting in the theatre. If an actor appears to be ignoring a cue light then it is best to cut it but after discussion with the actor concerned.

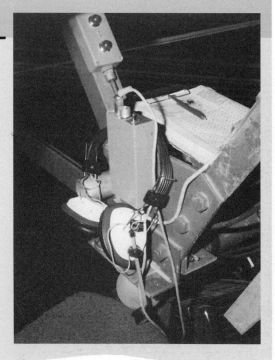

Cue lights and headsets set in a convenient if somewhat unusual position backstage.

Prompt desk before the cue lights are patched up and marked on the desk.

(Below) Prompt desk marked up and ready to start the technical.

theatre electricians if your theatre does not have a specific sound department. Stage management have to tell whoever rigs the equipment where they want headsets and where they want cue lights. Although it is often the case that the two go together this is not necessarily so. You will certainly need a set of headsets either side of the stage so that the rest of the team can contact the DSM especially if they are situated at the back of the auditorium. If there is flying in the show there will need to be a set on the fly floor and also in the follow spot positions if applicable. The sound and lighting board operators will also need a set each. Never assume that the headsets are there from the last production. Always make it very clear to the electricians how many sets you will need and where they should be positioned. Cue lights are needed wherever a technician or an actor will need to be cued either for an entrance or to carry out a technical cue. The standard cue lights for every show are the sound and lighting board operators, the fly floor and possibly for the follow spots. A cue light for actors depends very much on the individual actor and the design of the set. If an actor cannot see from the wings when his arch enemy has sipped the poisoned wine and he must not enter until the

133

man is dead then it is sensible for the DSM to cue the actor on once the other character has died.

Cue lights can be hung in almost any position you wish providing they are close to the action they are cueing and can be easily acknowledged. Anyone responding to a cue light must be able to still see it until after they have performed the cue. If you have to walk away from the cue light after acknowledging the standby in order to push a truck or do a scene change you must be able to see the green light otherwise the point is lost. The other rule with cue lights is that the audience in their normal enjoyment of the play must never see them. If a door is left open during the course of the action and the audience can clearly see a winking cue light then the cue light must be moved.

The DSM will also be required to tell the electricians in which order they want the prompt desk to be patched up. This is very important and working from left to right the order is as follows:

LX, SND, FLIES, followed by the next most frequently used cue light. They will vary for each production but are likely to be the cue lights for the scene changes, the most frequently used entrances or possibly the follow spots.

HEALTH AND SAFETY

Any action that has a health and safety issue related to it will have had the risk assessed by your production manager and/or the person responsible for health and safety in your theatre. These actions will require extra attention at the technical rehearsal and are often rehearsed first in full working light at a slower pace than the action calls for. When everyone concerned is comfortable with what they are doing and any problems have been resolved, the action will be performed in show lighting and at the required speed. You need to be familiar with all aspects of these actions including which other members of the company may be affected, perhaps because

they are doing a quick change in the wings at the time, in order that everyone and everything is included in rehearsing the action.

PUTTING CUES INTO THE BOOK

The DSM should be able to put some cues into the book during the rehearsal period. The script will often state the obvious such as, 'Mrs Jones crosses to the desk and switches on the lamp', that would be a cue to the LX board operator to bring up the desk lamp. There would be no cue numbers at this stage, but the DSM would know this was an LX cue point and write it lightly in pencil in the cue column and underline the action. The director might offer suggestions of cue points to the DSM such as, the opening of a scene to be early evening instead of the original written directions of moonlight, or the start of a sunset beginning at the top of a certain page and completing at the end of the scene. The director would ask for the note to be taken so that he could talk it over with the lighting designer during the

Patching the Desk

The order in which the cue lights are connected on the prompt desk will mirror the order the cues are written in the prompt book. A DSM should always stand the LX by first, followed by the SND and FLIES and then the cue lights particular to their production. Likewise a group of cues will always be called as LX first, followed by SND then FLIES and so on. If a sequence does not include a particular cue then it is obviously omitted but the order of the remaining cues keeps to this convention. Therefore the order in which the DSM asks operators to standby mirrors the order in which the cues will be called which, in turn, matches the order of the various switches on the prompt desk in front of them.

lighting session; the DSM would also mark this information into the cue column of their script.

Sometimes the creative teams will give the DSM a list of already planned cues and cueing points for their book, which can be of great help to the DSM and save a lot of time during a lighting or sound session. The lighting session is where most of the LX cues are given to the DSM, as each state is worked through so the cue points and their numbers are decided upon, also the DSM would put in their standbys for each cue or set of cues. Many other cues are also decided upon during the lighting sessions as each effect has a bearing on the other. For example, as a character makes for the exit, the LX cue is given; as the lights start to fade, the Fly cue is given, as the flown piece is half way in, the Sound cue is given; and by the time the lights, flies, and sound cues are completed the effect will look as if the transformation has all magically happened at the same time.

Sometimes cues are given together, for example a character's entrance, follow spot and fanfare have to coincide as one effect as the figure appears in the entrance. These would be the bracketed cues as in the illustration on page 137; most cue desks are equipped with a master switch to enable cue lights to be linked together.

The notation of the cues must be clear and easily read at a glance, so an abbreviated code is used: LX for the lighting cues – this is also a term used for almost anything to do with electrics including the personnel themselves; SND for the sound cues; FLY for anything flown in or out – this word in itself is already short enough. The capital letter Q can be used for 'cue' instead of taking up precious space in your cue column. Headsets rarely accompany the various off-stage cue lights, as the lights are used for actors' entrances or for crews who need to work on a scene change. Because there will only be one cue light down right and one down left, these cue lights will be used for many reasons during a show from an actor's entrance to a live gun-

Warnings by the DSM

Health and safety practice requires the DSM to warn the entire theatre via the tannoy system if loud bangs such as gunshots or explosions are about to occur on-stage. This must be done every time this action is rehearsed as well as each time it happens in performance. The announcement should be documented in the prompt copy to prevent it being missed if someone else covers for the DSM.

shot or door slam. However, the written cues in your script will often be as follows. SR Q light in brackets at the side of the SR will be a description of the use of that cue light – for example (Mr Smith enters) or (a gunshot). Often it may be clearer to write the effect only, such as Crash Go (SR Q light). The only word that should not be abbreviated is STANDBY. With a busy show you will need to see your cues coming. This word must stand out above the list of cues written, as if shortened it merges with the abbreviated list. List your cues in the order in which they happen (LX is usually at the top, but there are exceptions!); if the cues get cut or moved around during the technical, never alter the numbering. It is far too confusing for you and the operators. So it could read as LX Qs 7 8 9 10 14 16 17 because 11 12 13 and 15 are cut. Always make sure the numbers in the standby list are altered as well as the cue point. Mark this in your script as the changes happen or use your sticky notes, otherwise it will get forgotten.

The DSM will need to anticipate the cues. If the cues are neatly written and the lines to the text are straight and clear this will help you. To make sure this is clear to anyone who may have to pick up your script and run the show, always have your text on the right-hand side and the blocking and cue column on the left as you look

135

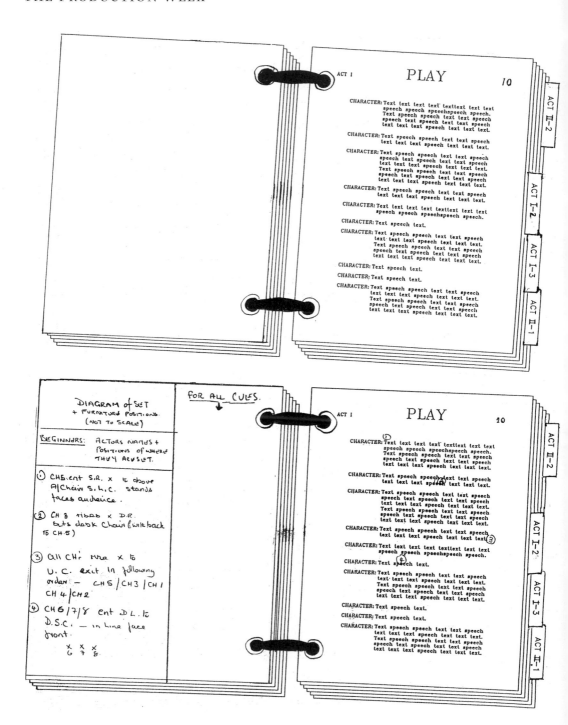

A prompt copy from blank play script to cues in the book.

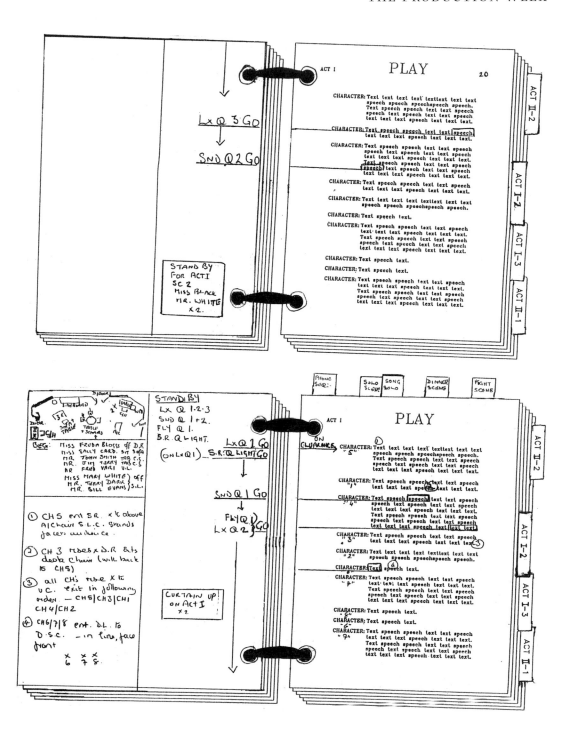

at the script. Make sure the text is always on that right-hand side all the way through the play.

The distance between a standby and a go is approximately 30 seconds. Should there be a lot of cues and single lines of text, then the standby could be as long as one and a half minutes. You would discuss this with the various technical areas before the technical rehearsal. It would not be fair to expect a flyman to be holding a rope for nearly two minutes before they fly something in. Try not to give standbys in the middle of a set of cues. It is confusing for the people on the other end of the headsets to hear this voice suddenly starting to stand someone by. Plus you could miss several cues while your attention has been interrupted.

The DSM must make sure they know why cues are happening. To be able to have good timing and sensitivity when cueing a show you must know the play and the cues thoroughly. The audience is a different crowd of people for every performance; their reactions to the play will therefore be different. The actors will find that the timings of some of their actions will also be different. Therefore the DSM must be aware of this, and in knowing the show have enough confidence to take their eyes off the book. Look at the stage as often as possible. It is no use cueing the LX operator to switch on a table lamp if the actor concerned is nowhere near it despite saying a line such as 'Shall I turn on the light?' even when the cue is written in the book to go on his line. Remember the performance is live and an actor will pace their performance according to the reaction they are getting from the audience. This may well affect the cueing of the show and a DSM needs to be alert to this by watching and listening to what is going on on-stage.

The DSM must maintain discipline not only with themselves but also with others. For example, never allow unnecessary chat over the headset, as cues can be missed and flying pieces could be mistimed which is foolish and

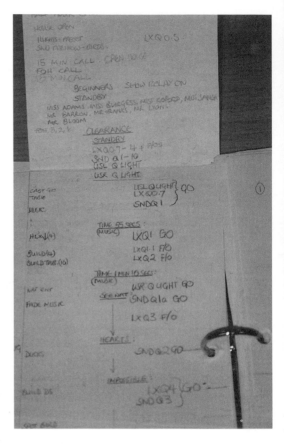

Opening sequence written out in the prompt copy with a flap to accommodate the extra number of cues found in an opening sequence.

dangerous. Do not discuss why a cue went wrong or did not happen, keep the show running and discuss during the interval or at the end of the performance. You need to be clear and consistent in the way you cue. Do not change the order of the cue lists in your script, or the calls to the company.

The DSM must always attend the actors' note session with the director. They follow the director's notes with the script, keeping to the correct scene and act as he talks. This way the DSM will be able to iron out some of the problems that may arise concerning cue positions and technical action for the actors, as they will have watched the show and been fully involved throughout. It may be that a cast member does not realize that a line or paragraph has been forgotten and that is why the cue did not happen, or perhaps it would be better to give the cue after the action, and not before or during it.

Never allow any actor or director near the microphone to give messages or bogus calls. Apart from being unprofessional this could be costly and potentially dangerous. An actor who had been allowed to give an emergency fire call over the tannoy to backstage as an April Fools' Day prank caused great panic and a lot of wasted time for the staff. In their haste to exit from the workshop, one of the staff dropped a pan of hot glue over their foot and ended up in A&E at the local hospital. The fire brigade also had to drive several miles in heavy traffic to reach the theatre, and all for nothing.

Always say 'please' and 'thank you' when cueing and giving calls. It makes you sound relaxed and confident and that is what the company and staff want to hear. Try not to make tannoy calls when you have been running to the microphone and are out of breath – all that is heard is a lot of heavy breathing and wheezing. Do not make a

call when you have been laughing hysterically, the voice comes across as giggly and as if you do not really mean what you are saying. If you make a call when you have just walked away from having a row with someone, you may sound very cross and unfeeling; this does not convey confidence to the company or technical teams.

During performances the DSM must make sure they are sitting at their desk from the half-hour call; this allows time to look at their book, collect their thoughts and forget the problems of the day. The DSM is also a point of contact for the SM should any emergency calls need to be made.

DRESS REHEARSALS

The complexity of the production and the timing of the previews and opening night will dictate the schedule and how much time there will be between the technical rehearsal and previews for the number of dress rehearsals. Sometimes the number will only be one DR or two at the most.

From the first dress rehearsal the stage management need to approach the production in performance mode. The SM will run the show from backstage, having cleared all the headsets, tables and so on from the auditorium. (The

A modern production desk in the stalls. All this needs to be removed before the first night; it is sometimes needed until after the final dress rehearsal.

production desk may be there for the first DR and removed for the final one.) The photographer will be in and set to take production shots for the FOH photo board. All costume, sound and LX cues should now be complete. The props should be set and checked and the wings swept and mopped or vacuumed, especially if carpet runners have been laid down. This is done to deaden the noise of busy feet from the cast and crews as they go about their business. There is always the comforting realization at the end of a dress rehearsal that there is still time to adjust or solve some of the problems that may arise, with the aim of getting it right on the first night.

SUPERSTITIONS

The theatre is steeped in superstition. Sayings have been handed down through the ages but many of the true meanings have been lost. Actors and sometimes directors have a lot of personal superstitions that have become a ritual wherever and whatever they are performing. It is important for the stage management to honour these wishes; indeed some of you may turn to lucky charms or rituals of your own before the opening night.

The following are some of the theatrical superstitions directors, actors, stage management, and often crews and technicians will believe very strongly.

1) Not to rehearse the curtain call until after the final dress rehearsal.
MEANING: Not known.
2) Not to say the last line of text in the final act until the first performance.
MEANING: Not known.
3) Not to use real flowers on stage.
MEANING: Because at the beginning of the 20th century an actress slipped and broke her ankle on the fallen petals from a bunch of real roses that had been set on stage.

4) Not to say 'Good Luck!' until the first night.
MEANING: Because it might tempt fate before the actual performance. There is a saying now to replace 'Good luck!' – that is, 'Break a leg' which originally came from the circus world and not the theatre.
5) Not to quote from 'Shakespeare's *Macbeth* or even mention the name when in the theatre and certainly not in performance.
MEANING: Because there are many words and quotes within the text that are black magic.
6) The colour green.
MEANING: Because it's a living colour and should be outside only, in plants and trees. On stage it is also meant to be a difficult colour to light.
7) Not to whistle in the dressing room.
MEANING: Unknown, it is thought to have derived from the meaning below.
8) Not to whistle back-stage.
MEANING: Because all the crews were men from the ships and the use of whistled orders on board became the same rule behind the scenes. So every time the flyman or crewman heard a whistle the scene was changed. Later it became dangerous to whistle out of turn.

The show will be timed act by act by the DSM and everyone will make necessary notes as they go of cues or props to be altered. At the end there will be a written report sheet, as there is for a performance that will start the check on the running times. There is a show report on each performance throughout the run of a production. This will be a constant update of how the show is proceeding, who may take over as understudy if required, the running times of the intervals and scene changes, and the playing time of the performers. In addition, the size of the audience, how well the show was received and how many curtain calls were made will be noted down.

OPPOSITE PAGE: *A show report.*

Opera Workshop
Show Report No. 4

Director: Stephen Medcalf   **Date:** Friday 14th July 2000

DSM: Julia Mathes   **Venue:** Linbury Studio

Performance No.: 2

	Time up	Time down	Running Time
Act I	19:15	20:32	1hr 17min
Interval	20:32	20:53	26mins
Act II	20:53	22:08	1hr 15mins
Total playing time			2hr 32mins
Total running time			2hr 58mins

Comments:

1. 10 minutes before the show the LX board operator noticed that the board had shut down. The workers were turned on, beginners were held for two minutes. The start of the show was delayed while attempts were made to reboot the board, and the stage manager made an on stage announcement to the public.
   At 7.15 the decision was taken to start the show in working light, and the director made an announcement to that effect. After five minutes of the show the board had rebooted and the correct states were brought up with the working lights still on.
   At the start of Oberon's aria the workers were switched off. However, because of the problems with the board (ethernet hub failure) the scrollers did not work throughout the show.
   The Opera House has called an engineer to fix the problem.

2. At the end of 'Midsummer Night's Dream' Mr. Vramsmo was very late for his cue to pick up his chair.

3. In LX Q23 (fluorescents on) they flickered and went out and then faded up. This happened every time they were used in act I. During the interval it was found that the load lamp had failed. Due to this the interval overran by 6 minutes. In 'Theodora' the fluorescents failed to come on on cue. They were wheeled in halfway through the recit. The problem was that because of work during the interval, they were still held out on the board.

4. LX Q67 (Build SL treads) was late – DSM error.

Lone Schacksen   Julia Mathes

Stage Manager   Deputy State Manager

Cc: Stephen Medcalf, Guiseppe di Ioria, Clive Timms, Sue Thornton, Peter Dean, PJ Booth, Conor McGivern, Steve Huttley, Nick Peel, Sue Hudson, Soozie Copley, Marion Marrs, Lone Schacksen, Julia Mathes, Sam Short, Angie Crockford, Production Notice Board (17).

11 FINAL STAGES OF THE PRODUCTION PROCESS

From the first dress rehearsal to the first night and sometimes even after that the director and the rest of the creative team will be giving notes to the company. The production is gradually coming together and during the dress rehearsals and previews the director and creative team are making their final adjustments. It is rare that any major changes will happen at this stage but there will be changes that affect stage management. These changes might include a change to an actor's entrance that in turn means a particular prop needs to be set in a different place backstage. You need to make sure that all your paperwork is kept up to date and setting lists and so on are amended to take account of these changes. The DSM will receive notes from the lighting designer and the director about the cueing of the show. They may need to change the position of some cues or adjust the timing when they are calling the cue. It may be that the blocking has changed in a particular scene and this changes the place in the script where the cue should be given. Any changes to the blocking or cuts to the text must be updated in the prompt copy. It is essential that you and your team keep accurate and up-to-date records of these changes. At this stage, setting lists, running copies, the prompt copy and also lighting and sound plots are constantly changing. You will not have time to type up all of these changes. It is much better that there are clear handwritten changes that are accurate and cur-

rent than a backlog of typing and therefore inaccurate lists from which to work. It is impossible to remember all these changes, most of which will be quite small, but it is very important that these notes are carried out as the creative team wish. They are refining the production and without these changes being implemented they cannot make progress to the finished production.

It is usual to have two dress rehearsals and sometimes you may have the luxury of three. In addition there will be at least one preview night – in the West End there may be three weeks of previews. A preview is a performance in front of a paying audience but without any press representatives casting a critical eye. It allows all concerned to experience an audience's reaction and particularly with a comedy can change an actor's timing for entrances, punch lines and pauses. Previews are also valuable for the DSM and the timing of the cues.

ORGANIZING PREPARATION TIME FOR THE SHOW

By now you will have a good idea of how long it takes to prepare for each performance. This is called setting up and means that all aspects of the production – for instance props, lighting, special effects and costume are in their starting positions ready to begin. For example props that are set in the stage right wing but at the end of the performance are left on-stage will be returned to the

This was one of many equally complicated scenes in this production of Road. *This production took well over an hour to set up. Guildhall School of Music and Drama, director Joseph Blatchley, Designer Geraldine Pilgrim, Lighting Designer Chahine Yavroyan.* Photo: Laurence Burns

correct wing. Each department is responsible for setting up or setting back their own aspects of the performance. For stage management this means setting back props and furniture, washing any used items such as glasses and plates and replacing burnt candles or torn envelopes. Every aspect of the show must be ready for the next performance and depending upon the complexity of the production this can take a minimum of an hour and often a lot longer.

Once you know how much time you need to set up, you can plan your team's time accordingly. Time on-stage is at a premium at this point in the production process and it is difficult to have

Thoroughly Checking All Departments

Whilst all the staging departments will set up for their own areas, as a stage manager you have ultimate responsibility if anything goes wrong during the performance. It is therefore worth diplomatically checking with each department that they have set up thoroughly and that all aspects of the show are working. A good example of this is to ask the LX department if they have checked the practical lamps on stage and are sure that when the actor mimes the switching on of the table lamp it will actually light up.

enough time to set up, have a meal break, allow the actors time on-stage to warm up their bodies and voices and give the lighting designer time to finish plotting the curtain call lighting. The production manager will be responsible for juggling all these conflicting requests for time on-stage but you can help them by staggering your team's meal breaks and being as quick and efficient as possible in setting up the show. This is quite a skill when you and your team are tired, hungry and still learning the inevitable last-minute changes to the setting lists, but with experience you learn ways in which this process can be safely speeded up enabling and you and your team to be ready on time for the next rehearsal.

One demand for time on-stage that remains after the opening night is time for the company to warm up on stage. Actors will warm up their voices and even their bodies almost anywhere but it is an enormous advantage to be able to warm up on-stage and test their voices in the auditorium in which they are about to play. Not all of the company will wish to do this but the opportunity for those who do should be available. When you are on tour it is essential that the company have time on-stage in the new venue and even if you are in your base theatre it is common for the whole company to be called to rehearse a dance routine or song before each performance.

PRODUCTION PHOTOGRAPHS AND PRESS CALLS

At some point between the end of the technical rehearsal and the first performance, production photographs will be taken. This usually happens during the final dress rehearsal but depends upon the director's preference and the photographer's availability. Production photographs are action shots taken during the dress rehearsal. They are then enlarged and used by the marketing department to publicize the production. The photographs will be mounted front of house and copies are also available for any local papers that may wish to include a photograph with their review. Good production photographers are extremely skilled professionals; many take these action shots as they happen without seeing any rehearsal beforehand. Stage management can be a great help in alerting the

photographer to particularly exciting moments or alternatively warning the photographer not to take shots of a certain scene because it would give the plot away. The predominant colour of the set is also useful to know as well as the point where any special effects such as smoke, haze or follow spots are used. As well as providing information for the photographer you must also remind the company that photographs will be taken at the next dress rehearsal. Usually it is clear in the production schedule when the photographer will be present but as with everything in this process, this is frequently subject to change. When it is known for sure that photographs will be taken, the DSM will announce this over the tannoy when they give the company call for that particular rehearsal. They should remind the company that all elements of their costume should be worn including wigs and make-up. Actors very often wear an uncomfortable piece of costume only once during the production week and don't bother with make-up after technical rehearsal, but they would not wish to be photographed in this state!

Sometimes the press or your own marketing department need specific shots that are almost posed for the camera. They may be writing a specific piece about the imminent production and require shots of a particular actor or scene to accompany their copy. In this instance you may be asked to re-create a specific scene then another immediately after. Invariably these scenes are not chronological and stage management need to employ all their continuity skills to make sure that each snap shot scene is accurate as far as costume, props and set are concerned.

A VISIT FROM THE FIRE OFFICER

Before the first public performance it is very common to have a visit from your local fire officer. The fire officer is responsible for making sure that nothing happens in the theatre either on-stage or front of house that will endanger

A busy theatre foyer at Salisbury Playhouse showing production photographs for the pantomime in the background.

The chorus of **The Tsarina's Shoes** *carrying candles. The use of candles is not automatically forbidden. You should consult the fire officer for your theatre giving him details of exactly how the candles will be used.*

the public. They work closely with the licensing authorities and have the power to stop a show even in performance if they believe that a dangerous situation is occurring. You and the production manager need to have developed a good working relationship with your local officer and have discussed any potential problems well in advance of the technical rehearsal. These professionals can be very skilled in helping you to achieve apparently dangerous effects without actually putting anyone at risk.

They have the power to make spot checks to ensure that you are carrying out their recommendations and if not they can close the show. Certain standards must be met as a matter of course when building sets for the theatre and all materials must be fireproofed. This is a very specialist area and you must take advice from the fire officer or other qualified professional if you are in any doubt about the safety of a particular prop or piece of furniture. Fire Officers have been known to walk onto a set to test that any material on the stage does not ignite within a certain number of seconds when they hold a lighter to it. In practice if you have established a good working relationship with the fire authorities you will not be subjected to these spot checks for every performance, as they will have confidence in your attitude to health and safety. As a stage manager you must take this aspect of your job seriously and work with the authorities in ensuring that your theatre, set and stage are safe places to work.

145

12 FROM THE FIRST NIGHT TO THE FINAL CURTAIN

KEEPING THE SHOW POLISHED

After the enjoyable but hard and tiring rehearsal period passes, the first night arrives. The adrenalin flows, 'Good Luck' cards are opened, bouquets of flowers arrive at the stage door for the company, the stage management bustle around calling out last-minute shout checks and hunt for vases or jam jars for all the flowers, the dressers set the costumes in the quick-change areas and answer frantic calls from the dressing rooms to 'Zip me up please and can you help with my wig?' Friends and relatives belonging to the actors are chased from the dressing rooms. The director is trying to give last-minute notes to the actor who is making throaty humming noises and doing stretching exercises outside their dressing room. The half-hour call is heard over the tannoy, the bustle slows down; only the actors now seem to be in their dressing rooms; and the ASM checks personal props. The stage manager gives a final check of the stage to see that all working lights are out, no brooms are left leaning against the proscenium arch, then to the auditorium to check that all drapes are hanging straight and set on their correct dead, that the auditorium working lights are out. When the stage manager is satisfied that everything is in order, they would then hand the house over, by telling the Front of House manager that the house is now theirs. This means that everything is ready and the house can now be open to the public. The Front of House manager gives his ushers and doormen a signal for the auditorium doors to open, and the public start to take their seats and the countdown to the first performance begins.

A decision is made by the director together with the stage manager, on the most suitable point in the play when latecomers can be allowed to take their seats. The Front of House manager would organize suitable seats that were unobtrusive and easy to find in the darkness of the auditorium.

Backstage it is now time for the beginners' call, there is more humming and stretching from the cast, shouts of 'Break a leg!' echo

Stuart Tucker cueing Grand Hotel *in a performance by the Guildhall School of Music and Drama.*

down the dressing room corridors. The company take their positions, the auditorium doors close, the DSM is given the signal for the first cue, the lights dim, a hush descends over the auditorium and the play begins.

The last curtain call, thunderous applause, a lot of giggles as the cast now release all their tensions, calling out thank you to the crew and stage management as they all make for their dressing rooms. Before all the equipment is switched off, the DSM will announce the running times of each act followed by the next day's performance time plus any note sessions or company warm-ups that may be scheduled. They will also ask around the technical areas for any notes that may need to be reported on the show report sheet, for example why LX Q 25 was late – whether it was owing to equipment or operator error and so on. The stage manager and team will be putting valuable props away in the production manager's safe, washing up all the china and glassware, covering up the props remaining on the prop tables and sweeping up any broken items left on stage. Maybe there has been a confetti drop or possibly a fight and there is a lot of stage blood spilled on the beautifully painted floor. The stage manager will run off copies of the show report sheet and distribute to all the technical departments, so they can be read first thing in the morning and if possible any repairs or faulty mechanics can be put right. The director can see if there were any serious faults with the running times of the acts and will address this at the note session before the second night's performance. Finally the show has ended and the stage management can now relax, change out of their stage management blacks and make for the pub or the first-night party.

Everyone needs to be alert and very much on their guard for what is known in the theatre as a second-night performance. Both the company and the stage management will be tired after the energies of the evening before, plus the effects of the after-show party. This often means the performances may be low key with some of the sequences badly timed or lines forgotten. The DSM will also need to be alert as they may lose concentration and miss cues. The audience will be without the company's relatives, friends and first-night supporters so will probably come across as quiet, slow and unappreciative. The stage manager must encourage everyone to find as much of that first-night bubble as they can.

Once the opening night has passed, the stage management must also prepare for the possibility of someone in their team being ill or off during one of the future performances. They should all learn each other's jobs. The company manager should learn the SM's running list, the stage manager the DSM's script and cueing sequences, both perhaps to run one of the matinée performances. The ASMs need to learn each other's sides plus their setting and running lists.

DEALING WITH ALL EVENTS THAT MAY ARISE

Stage managers often have to deal with the unexpected during the run of a production. For example there may be a phone call, while you are in rehearsal for the next production, saying your leading lady has developed laryngitis over the week-end and cannot perform that evening. Her husband is not sure how long she will be away, but will keep you informed. You would then contact your production secretary and the director who would try to find a replacement. Most repertory companies do not have understudies unless you have quite a large cast in which case it may be possible for a small part player to cover a couple of the lead characters; this is usual with Shakespeare plays and musicals. The stage manager would phone around the existing cast and explain there was to be a rehearsal call that afternoon to put in the replacement for the evening show. This replacement could be someone who would be available to play the part, but would need to perform while reading the script, or it may be someone who has been in the same play recently playing the same character and would therefore know the lines. The production manager and crew would need to be informed and stage management would have to leave the rehearsals for the next show. The wardrobe would need to be alerted in case alterations to the costume were necessary. The box office would need to know so as to inform the public that they would be seeing a different actress that evening. The Front of House manager would then slip the programmes with the name of the new actress.

The stage manager needs to make sure that the pace and standards of the show are kept up throughout its run and that all the props and technical effects are repaired or replaced if necessary. The stage must be kept tidy and clean. Should the director or an agent make a spot visit to the show, it must look as slick and new as it did on the first night.

There are those nights when you hope the director, or maybe an agent is not out front – such as the night the telephone was left off the desk on-stage, by a forgetful member of the stage management team during a scene change, the phone bell rang, the actor put his hand out for the phone, found nothing, bell kept ringing and the actor frantically began looking around the set. The doorbell rings, the actor goes to answer the door, to discover a quick-thinking ASM wearing a borrowed cap and jacket from a crew member, standing there holding a telephone (still ringing! the DSM in their panic kept their finger on the bell), 'I've come to fit your phone sir', moves to the desk, pretends to plug it in, touches his cap and exits. The phone stops ringing, the actor answers it, the scene continues. Apparently not many people in the audience noticed anything amiss!

The company manager would make sure that they watched scenes from the back of the auditorium each evening. If possible the stage manager would try and swap places with the CM for a few of the evenings, so they could also watch the show from the front. It is a good place to view the performances and the presentation of the stage, to see if those small jobs such as the broken door handle or window catch have been attended to? Or that the trimming on the chair has been stuck down? Have the bottoms of the table and chairs been dusted?

The stage may be used continuously during the day once a show has opened. If there is a rehearsal of the next show taking place on stage, you must make sure that the team working on that rehearsal does not use your furniture and props or put dirty footprints on the nice white material covering the sofa; or move the props, and leave them scattered around the wings or worse, actually break one of them and neglect to tell you, with the result that it does not get discovered until the half-hour call of the evening show.

There may be press calls and photo shoots to organize for the evening show and the one in rehearsal that will be requested to take place on stage, often not releasing the stage until an hour after the time you have planned to set up for the evening performance.

The final performance arrives, followed by the get out. Stage management clear the stage and wings of all their props and furniture. Borrowed and hired items get cleaned, washed, packed and labelled ready to be returned first thing on Monday morning. The theatre stocks of props and furniture are cleaned and washed and put away in the props and furniture stores. Finally a very tired stage management team crawl home to bed to dream of the next show opening at the end of the following week. It is almost time to close the production file on this show but not until you are certain that all your borrowed and hired items are safely returned, your petty cash complete and all the invoices deposited with the finance department. One show has closed and it's straight into a production week before the next first night!

That's what stage management is about!

GLOSSARY

Acts a) Divisions of a play, usually with an interval between the first and second division; b) a performance by an individual artiste in variety theatre.

Acting Area The area inside the set where the action takes place.

Act Drop The tabs or a cloth dropped at the end of an act.

Anticipate Giving a cue a fraction early to enable the operators to receive the information and put it into effect, and the cue to happen at the precise moment required.

Apron The extension in front of the stage. During the Elizabethan era the extension used to be curved rather like an apron, hence the name.

ASM Assistant Stage Manager.

Backing Scenery behind an opening, such as an arch, window or doorway.

Bar Flown metal tubular bar from which scenery or stage lights are suspended.

Batten Lengths of timber at the tops and bottoms of cloths.

Battening Out Timber used for joining two or more flats together for flying.

Beginners Actors required in the first scene of Act One or Act Two called by the DSM five minutes before the curtain goes up (usually anyone who makes an entrance or is on stage during the first five minutes of the action).

Bible The book, the prompt copy. Because it has absolutely every detail of the show written into it, it is often called the Bible.

Blacks a) The complete black outfit worn by the stage management and crew who appear on stage in dim lighting to change the scene; b) black masking to hide the wings or piece of scenery from the audience; c) a set of tabs.

Black Box The stage with no scenery. A black painted floor, black legs on each side of the stage, and black tabs up stage on the further most flying bar, and black borders. This provides a black box effect when you view it from the front. Usually used for experimental performances.

Bleedthrough Light brought up on stage to present a scene behind a gauze.

Blinder Black drapes that back a gauze to prevent a bleedthrough of light too early.

Boards A term sometimes used to mean the stage, hence the expression 'Tread the boards'.

Book A term used for the prompt copy, hence the expression 'On the book'.

Book Flat A pair of scenic flats hinged together. Often used behind a door-opening as masking. They are usually small, and useful when touring, or in a small space.

Borders Lengths of material hung horizontally across stage to mask lighting bars or tops of scenery. Usually black, but can be coloured to suit the design. Sometimes these borders are hard, framed or made of board and cut to a shape.

Box Set A set consisting of three walls (audience being the fourth wall) with doors and windows, and a ceiling piece.

Brace *See* Stage Brace.

Brail To pull one corner or side of a cloth or flown flat upstage or downstage from its original position by means of a length of sash line either at the top or bottom of the suspended item to prevent the next flown piece or lighting bar tangling with it.

149

Breast To have a length of hemp (*see also* Hemp) between the stage right and left fly floor in front of or behind the flying lines of the suspended piece, to enable clearance for other flying pieces or make a space for a person to walk from one side of the stage to the other.

Build a) Constructing the set in the workshop; b) to fade up with a light cue gradually over several minutes, example, LX Q 24 build over 3 minutes; c) raise the volume of sound with an effects cue.

Call Notification of a time when an actor is called for a rehearsal or to a wardrobe fitting or a musician to a band call, etc.

Call Board A board positioned usually near a stage door, where company information is posted, such as rehearsal calls, etc.

Cans Headsets with a single earpiece and small microphone attached, used by the DSM and technical operators when running a show.

Canvas Heavy duty cotton fabric used for covering wooden frames to create 'scenic flats'. This method is used less and less, as flats now tend to be made of ply (sometimes using the canvas over the top of the ply to add texture to a design).

Casuals People who are employed on occasions only when required, to work a show or for a fit-up/get-out.

Catwalk A narrow walkway often attached to the front of the stage to bring action out into the audience (rather like a fashion show).

Centre Line An imaginary line from the front to the back of the stage from an exact centre position between the proscenium arch.

Centre Stage The centre of the acting area.

Chalk Line *See* Snap Line.

Choreographer A person who creates the staging of dance in a musical or ballet.

Clear a) To remove all props and furniture from the stage; b) to instruct all the actors to move from the stage; c) to switch all switches back to neutral on a lighting board or cue desk.

Clearing Stick A very long lightweight wooden or bamboo pole used for clearing a piece of scenery or cloth that has tangled with another.

Cleat To tie two flats together edge to edge.

Cleat Hook Shaped piece of metal for tying off a rope line, usually found on a fly floor or on the back of scenic flats.

Cleat Line A sash line fixed to the top of the back of a scenic flat, and when bringing the two flat edges together, the sash is thrown over the top cleat hook, pulled tight so there is not a gap at the join, and the sash is then tied off on a double cleat hook at waist height of the flat.

Cloth A large area of painted cloth to whatever the scene demands. The cloth is then battened top and bottom and finally suspended from a flying bar. Sometimes it is not battened, but has ties attached to the top which tie to the flying bar where it hangs and there is a metal tubular conduit or chain threaded through the hem of the cloth to weight it.

Conduit The narrow tubular hollow metal lengths that cover electrical wires in permanent installations, but usually used as above for weighting the bottoms of cloths or gauzes.

Control Box The closed-off area at the back of the stalls or circle from where the LX board operator works the show. The DSM often cues the show either in the same area or in an adjoining room.

Comps Free tickets for agents/managements/friends of the cast, and trades from whom you may have borrowed a lot of props.

Creative Team The team of people consisting of director/designers (scenic, costume, lighting, sound), choreographer, who between them create the whole presentation of the show.

Crew Technicians who operate all the technical areas on stage during a show.

Cross Over A pathway furthest up-stage of the set that is masked from the audience, to allow the company and stage management to cross the stage from left to right without being seen.

Cue The signal that tells the technicians and the actors when to make the set change, the sound or the entrance happen and to bring the lights up or down on a scene.

Cue Light The light used to signal the person required to take action, e.g. red light for 'Stand By', green light for 'Go'.

Cue Sheet A list made in numerical order of actions made on cue.

Cue to Cue a) When the director and lighting designer work through the script with the DSM putting all the cue points in the book; b) cutting cue to cue in a technical rehearsal leaving out as much of the text and action as possible to save time.

Curtain Large suspended heavyweight fabric drapes. House curtain (or tabs), front curtain (or tabs) used to divide the audience from the stage. Sometimes lighting is used instead of the house curtain.

Curtain Call The line up of the actors to take the bow to the audience at the end of the show. This used to be taken with house curtain (tabs) coming in at the end of each bow, but now it is more likely to be with a lighting blackout at the end of each bow.

Curtain Up The beginning of the performance. Even when there is no curtain, just lights up, the term 'curtain up on act one' given by the DSM over the tannoy is still used as it is universally understood.

Cyclorama (Cyc) Plain cloth or plastic at the back of the stage that extends around the sides that gives the feeling of space. The term is sometimes used for a straight sky cloth (blue painted cloth) hung on the furthest bar US. In some of the older theatres with small stages the back wall is painted white or blue and known as the cyc.'.

Dead a) The taped mark on the rope of a flying piece that determines the height of the flown item. There is also a mark for flying something out, it has 'an out dead'; b) any truck or revolve position has a marked dead, take the truck to its off dead' or on stage dead'; c) props, costume, light, or sound FX that is no longer required. 'kill that light, that light is dead'. 'That prop is no longer needed it is now dead'.

Dead Line To make the deadline of when a drawing or design has to be reached. Also finding a prop or making up working lists all have a deadline of when they should be completed.

Deck Old fashioned term used for the stage, 'bring it in to the deck'.

Designer Part of the creative team, the one who makes the visual part of the show; in the case of the sound designer the oral part of the production. (Separate designers for the following: Set/Costume/Lighting/Sound.)

DLP Dead Letter Perfect, 'know your lines'. An old-fashioned term still used today.

Door Slam Device used to simulate the sound of a door slamming off stage. Usually a small door in a frame or mounted on a box to give it more depth of noise, this has locks, bolts bells and door knockers attached, which are rung or slammed on cue. The door slam can also be a piece of wood (3 × 1) which is held at one end by the foot, and the other end by the hand then slammed on the floor at the relevant time.

Down Centre Stage The area nearest the tab line, along the invisible centre line.

Downstage Anywhere below the original point. Downstage of the table, downstage of the arm chair, the downstage end of the counter, etc.

Dressings Any item that dresses the set and is not handled by the characters in the play, for example cushions, ornaments, rugs and curtains, pictures etc.

Dry For an actor to forget their lines.

DSM Deputy Stage Manager.

Effects (or Fx) Any simulation of an oral or visual or magical and sometimes pyrotechnics effect that appears as real as possible.

Electrics (or LX) a) The technicians who handle all things electric; b) any electrical equipment from a plug to the lanterns.

Entrance a) The doorway or opening allowing a person onto the stage; b) an actor making an entrance onto stage from any off-stage position.

Exterior The backing to an outside world through a door or window, or it maybe a scene that is an exterior setting.

False Proscenium (or False Prosc.) A specially built section to set behind the actual proscenium that can either make the proscenium narrower, or it may be a specially designed piece for the show.

Fire Proofing Most items used on stage are made from already fire-proofed materials. Should anything not be treated there are fireproofing solutions available.

Fit-Up Putting the set on stage and assembling to the design, flying necessary pieces, building composite sections and trucks etc.

Flats Wooden frames covered with scenic canvas, treated and painted/textured accordingly. Flattage these days are more likely to be made of ply, with possibly canvas covering the ply to form a texture before painting.

Flipper A flat hinged to another to flip out and form an extra piece of scenery or perhaps to support the other flat without using extra bracing.

Float a) To float a flat by gently letting it fall to the stage allowing the air trapped under the main body of the flat to soften the fall; b) the term used for the old-fashioned footlights that used to be on the edge of the stage. (Originally footlights used to be wicks floating in oil, hence the name float or floats). Can also be a term used for the small microphones laid along the edge of the stage for pantomimes and musicals.

Floor Cloth A heavy duty cloth (rather like a tarpaulin) usually painted as part of the design, sometimes the set will be built on top of the cloth or it may be cut to the shape and size of the acting area.

Flying Bar Metal tubular bars that scenery is suspended from by ropes or chains depending on the weight, then pulled up via the counterweight ropes.

Fly Floor A platform at the side of the stage running up and down stage. The flying lines and breaks are operated from this platform or walkway.

Flyman Person who operates the flying lines.

Flies The area above the stage that holds all the suspended scenery away from the audience's view.

Fluff To muddle and stumble over words in a speech.

Fold Back Speakers at the side of the stage, usually just above the proscenium arch. The pit is mic'd and the cast are able to hear certain instruments clearly.

Foot Someone placing a foot against the bottom of a flat to prevent it slipping while another walks the flat up from the top.

Forestage A true forestage is the small area in front of the tab line where the footlights used to be, but today the apron tends to be called the forestage.

Fourth Wall Within a box set the fourth wall is the audience, however it can also apply to the acting area's fourth side.

Foul When two items become entangled with each other, whether it is flown or scenery on stage that is being moved.

French Brace A triangular fixed brace attached by hinge or fixed to the back of a flat.

Front Cloth A painted cloth (part of a design) that hangs on the bar as far down stage near the house tabs as possible.

Front of House (FOH) Anything that is on the audience side of the proscenium arch from foyer to auditorium.

Full Stage A scene using the whole available space.

FUF Full up to Finish. Meaning stage lighting up to full for the curtain calls.

Gauze An open-weave, net-like fabric which becomes transparent when lit from behind.

Get-In Unloading the built set pieces from the workshop to the stage. Also another name for the dock doors through which the load passes.

Get-Off The ramp or treads behind the set that help actors to exit from an upper level of the set.

Get-Out The reverse of Get-In.

Glass Crash A live sound FX made by using a large strong box containing broken glass that enables a person to pour a bucket of glass into the box to make the sound of breaking windows.

Go The action word for a cue.

Green A word used for stage, 'see you all tomorrow on the green', another old-fashioned term still used. On the green came from the days when they laid green baize, a felt-like material (as a billiard table), on the stage to prevent the costumes getting ruined by the dirty floors which were often covered in sawdust.

Green Room The green room is an actors' rest room, where they can drink coffee and doze between acts. It derived from China many centuries ago when their rest areas were outside with plenty of greenery growing around the walls; as life moved on the rooms became interiors and the walls were painted a very pale green, rather like hospitals and doctors waiting rooms today. Green is said to be a restful, calming colour.

Grid The metal girders forming the slatted ceiling above the stage, above which all the pulleys are rigged so the lines are able to drop through the slats and attach to the flying bars.

Ground Plan The plan of the set drawn to scale showing the position of the set and flying bars.

Ground Row (Electrics) A row of lights on the floor below a cloth or cyc (or scenic ground row) shining light across the cloth to the middle line, the top lights then cross over that middle line, fusing the two sets of lights.

Ground Row (Scenic) The scenic ground row is usually a low cut-out of fields or houses in perspective to dress the outside of a window, or hide the bottom of the cyc if it's a full stage. It also hides the LX ground row!

Half The half-hour call which is called thirty-five minutes before the curtain-up time.

Hand Cue Using a hand signal instead of a cue light, especially good when there are not enough cue lights or they suddenly stop working! The hand goes stiffly up above your head, and drops cleanly when the cue point arrives. These signals must be clear and not muddled in any way. In the very dark wings it is a good idea

to wear a white glove, then the signal can be seen clearly.

Hand Props All small items handled by the actors, carried on and off stage are called hand props. This word derived from David Garrick, the famous actor of a century or more ago. In Garrick's day props were not used a great deal, but he liked them and started to use them for every part he played. He used his own things and marked them all as the property of David Garrick. This was the start of the word 'prop', and over time the term evolved to become 'hand prop'.

Hanging Plot List of all flown items and what bar they are on.

Heads A warning that must be shouted from the fly floor during fit-up/strike and during technical rehearsals to warn anyone who maybe in the way. For example 'HEADS DOWN STAGE cloth coming in' or 'HEADS CENTRE STAGE flat going out!'.

Health & Safety Keeping strictly to all the health and safety regulations, and risk assessments associated with a production.

Hemp Rope of various thicknesses used for flying.

House The term for the auditorium and the audience. 'What are the house like tonight?' is a well-known question during the run of a show.

House Tabs The drapes, usually heavy red velvet with gold fringing attached, that divide the audience from the stage.

In Can you bring the cloth for act two IN?

Inset An area inside the main set used for another part of a building by either a free-standing flat with a chair and table set in front of it or a truck or a flown flat. Whatever the design, it is a set within the main set ... an INSET!

In the Round An acting area set with the audience on four sides, sometimes with a low cut-away set to prevent masking the actors from the audience. This four-sided area does not have to be circular, as long as the audience are seated on all four sides it is known as in the round.

Iron The well-known word for Safety Curtain.

Island Setting A setting that is set centre stage with no masking or apparent ways on and off the set, hence island setting.

Kill To make a prop or light dead, i.e. needed anymore.

Lantern A window-like construction above the grid which is able to open once the lever at the side of the stage (next to the safety curtain buttons) is pulled in the event of a fire on stage, this would cause a draught tunnel sucking the flames up through this window, preventing it spreading elsewhere.

Lead The main part in a show, leading actress/actor or lead part.

Legs The vertical soft black drapes at the side of the stage masking the wings from the audience. Can be of a lighter colour or coloured to fit the design, but usually black.

Levels a) Levels of a set made from different-sized steel deck; b) levels for recorded sound FX – 'a levels session'.

Lines a) Flying lines; b) learning one's lines.

Live a) Live performance; b) live sound FX.

LX An abbreviation of the word electrics, especially for the book.

Marie Tempest Door-closing device named after the lady who devised it, an actress who worked at the end of the 19th century, known for her musical comedy timing.

Marking a) A rehearsal run without emotion, just marking it for the moves or action; b) putting the marks on stage (small as possible) behind the feet of furniture.

Mark Out To mark out the perimeters of the set from the ground plan given to the stage management by the designer, by sticking down coloured plastic tape.

Masking Using black drapes or material to mask anything not wanted to be seen by the audience.

Milking It Over-playing the applause, especially the curtain call. Always leave the public wanting more, not wait until there are just a couple of pairs of hands clapping.

Model Box A model of the set made by the designer and presented inside a model box of the theatre.

Multiple Set A set designed as a composite of static areas on stage, for example showing a living room/kitchen/bedroom/and garden, sometimes used for simultaneous action.

Nautical Many centuries ago all the workers behind the scenes were employed from the ships that docked in the various towns and cities. They brought with them a lot of nautical terms and superstitions, such as rigging, canvas, deck, boards, brailing, breasting, etc. The famous superstition is whistling, this is still unlucky for a sailor at certain times during their work aboard. Plus the fact that they used whistling to change the set, which meant, if it was done out of turn the set would be changed when they were not ready for it to happen.

Off An actor missing their entrance is known as off.

Off Stage The wings; anything that may be set or may be cued off stage.

On Stage The actor or the call will be on stage.

On Stand By You are on Stand By for the next cue.

On the Book The DSM is on the book.

OP Opposite prompt.

Open Stage/Set There is no set for the next production – it is an open set or stage.

Orchestra Pit The lower level in front of the stage where the orchestra are positioned to play for a musical or opera. Many centuries ago it was the pit where in the intervals between the acts they used have bear bating and cock fights. After the animal sport they were replaced with musicians and the stalls for seating was set very close to the orchestra so extending the pit space; these were known (some old theatres still have this marked on their seating plans) as the pit stalls.

OTT Over the top, especially with a bit of stage business.

Out Fly the piece out.

Out Front An actor will be asked to look out front or face out or front.

Pack Stacking a load of flats, back to back and face to face against the wall in the wings.

Paper the House To fill the house with an audience holding complimentary tickets.

Pass Door The door that leads from back stage to the auditorium.

Periaktoi Triangular scenic sections which can rotate to show different scenes.

Personal Props Any small item that may be worn or put into a pocket is a personal prop. A watch/handkerchiefs/purses/wallets/cigarettes/matches/lighters, etc.

Picture Frame Stage A proscenium arch stage presentation.

Plot To plot which cues go where. This may be lights/flics/sound or stage.

Press Call A call made between the publicity/marketing personnel and the local or national press, to take a rehearsal or stage photograph of the cast.

Preview A performance given to the public who have been given reduced seat prices or complimentary tickets, knowing the show will still be gaining the final polish before the press and the first night of possible managements and agents in the audience.

Production Desk The long table in the stalls throughout the technical and dress rehearsals. This long table has the lighting designer and board operator sitting at it plus the director and set designer and often the production manager. All the communications equipment and the lighting consul will be in operation.

Production Manager A person responsible for the workshop/paintshop/wardrobe/lighting department/sound and casual labour for productions, as well as the budget/scheduling, running fit-ups and get-outs.

Prompt Copy The book in which all the moves the actors make are entered during the rehearsal period. At a later date the cues get notated also. Known as the 'Bible'.

Prompt Corner The corner from where the show will be cued by the DSM, it is situated in the wings at the side of the stage. This area can be stage right or left, depending on the theatre and its availability of the correct sockets for the desk.

Prompt Desk The desk that incorporates all the cue lights, call facilities, relay of show switch, telephones, stop watches. Used by the DSM.

Prompter A person who calls out the word or line an actor forgets. Often the DSM's job as well as to cue the show. Because they will have been in the rehearsals, and know the actors and show well. There are some companies who are able to spare a stage management person to just prompt.

Prop Table A table laid with white paper, and each individual prop drawn around, set out in scenes and acts. Use of white paper makes it possible for the actors to find the prop in the very dark wing area.

Proscenium Arch (Prosc.) The picture-frame effect behind which is the stage, this arch frames the setting.

PS Prompt Side.

Pyrotechnics (Pyros) The bangs, explosions and firework FX often worked electrically by the electricians or a special effects person.

Q The abbreviation of cue used in the prompt copy and on cue sheets.

Quarter The fifteen-minute call, as the countdown nears beginners.

Quick Change A costume change that has to be achieved in either thirty seconds or one minute.

Quick Change Area An area set out in the wings for the above to happen, with mirror/table and chairs, surrounded by flats to make for some privacy.

Repertory A theatre that runs a permanent company of actors. They perform so many plays in a season of several months. Once each production runs and ends it is never brought back, and while the play is in production there is another in rehearsal and another in the planning process.

Repertoire A set-up of plays which alternate in the run of weeks and sometimes months of a season. These shows can be stored and taken out of the repertoire if they are not selling well or the actors have other commitments.

Répétiteur Pianist for opera and musical rehearsals.

Revolve A large circular disc on stage that rotates either clockwise or anti-clockwise, on which there are several settings.

Rigging (To Rig) The LX hang all the required lanterns for a production, the sound will set up all their necessary equipment and speakers.

Right Stage right.

Rostrum (Rostra) The various stage levels made of steel deck to elevate scenes or actors.

Run-through A run of the whole play in the rehearsal room using all the actual or stand-in props and furniture, stopping if possible at only the plotted intervals.

Runner a) The carpet laid down in the wings to deaden the sound of footsteps; b) an ASM who is not designated to any particular wing or area back stage, during a show; c) lightweight curtains usually without a split in the centre, that run across stage from left to right by someone (pulling) running them across by hand or on a tab track.

Running Order A list of titled scenes and or songs in order.

Running List A list laid out in order, of all the cues and events that have to be worked through on a show.

Safety Curtain The heavy fire-resistant iron curtain attached to the proscenium arch, that when in use prevents a fire spreading either back to the front or front to the back of the stage and auditorium. This would enable the audience and or back-stage people to escape safely.

Sandbag A canvas bag weighted with sand with a metal ring attached to the top, to enable it to be hung from free hemp lines to prevent them slipping through the pulleys.

Scene Change A planned action of stage management and crew to change from one scene to another as quietly and discretely as possible.

Scene Drop a) A passage of time between scenes, this may include a change of props or settings; b) a cloth that denotes a specific scene, and is dropped in at the end of a scene.

Schedules A written plan of work needing to be done from the strike of one show to the fit-up, technical and dress rehearsals to the opening night of the next.

Set a) The design, a set that is built and put onto the stage for the actors to act in and the whole is presented to the audience; b) all props and furniture are set on stage; c) when all the operators are set and ready to go, or everyone has set back to the previous scene.

Set Piece A piece of free-standing scenery.

Setting Line The designed line, usually painted. Often its position is US of the proscenium arch and tab line from where the set position is measured (sometimes this setting line can be as far down as the edge of stage or onto the apron.

Sightlines A line that limits the vision of the audience from the far side seats of an auditorium, and height should the theatre have a circle and upper circle. Also making sure there is a line marked on the floor in the wings up to (and not past) the point where the audience is still invisible to the actor and the actor invisible to the audience.

Sitzprobe An opera and musical term used when the cast sing along with the full orchestra, but do not act.

Snap Line A container that holds a length of string and loose chalk dust. The chalk dust when the container is shaken covers the string, the string is then pulled out and held taught by two people at opposite ends of the measured area, then snapped against the floor; a chalk line appears on the floor ready to mark with sticky tape slightly above or below (otherwise the chalked surface will not allow the tape to stick!).

Snow Bag A snow effect. A flown canvas trough-like bag with slits cut in the canvas, the bag is filled with the specially bought fireproofed paper snow flakes and the bag is flown out. On cue the bag is jiggled about and the snow falls through the slits.

Sound Designer Someone who designs all the sound FX and music for a show.

Spike To fix by a nail, or a nail itself.

Spot Line A temporary line dropped from the grid (not on a pulley) to suspend an object such as a ceiling light in an exact position.

Stage Left Prompt side. The left-hand side of the stage from an actor's view.

SM Stage Manager.

Stage Right Opposite prompt. The right-hand side of the stage from an actor's point of view.

Stage Cloth *See* Floor Cloth.

Stage Weight An iron weight which is put on the metal plate at the bottom of an extending brace to hold it and the flat in place when the brace is attached.

Stand By A warning given by a light and verbally to operators and actors before they are given the 'Go' on cue.

Strike To strike, get rid of the set or props when changing a scene, or getting rid of the set at the end of a show's run.

Tabs A set of drapes used as the front curtain dividing the audience from the stage or as drapes to divide the stage into acting areas, especially in pantomimes and musicals and operas when a scene would be set behind the mid-stage tabs.

Tag The last line of a play or scene or a variety artists gag (joke). The tag line.

Tallescope A metal adjustable vertical ladder on wheels with a platform at the top.

Tannoy A calling system used by the DSM at their desk to call the actors to the stage when required.

Thunder Sheet A metal sheet with a handle on the bottom, which is suspended by its top somewhere in the wings. At a given cue the sheet is rattled by holding the handle at the bottom of the sheet and a thunderous noise ensues.

Tie Off To tie off a cleat line.

Topping And Tailing *See* Cue to Cue.

Treads A set of steps.

Truck A platform on wheels.

Up Centre Stage At the furthest point away from the audience towards the centre of the back of the stage.

Walk Down The staircase walked down by the cast for a curtain call in a pantomime or musical, usually with specifically designed costumes for the occasion.

Walk It Up *See* Foot.

Wardrobe The department where all the costumes are made.

Wardrobe Chart A graph showing all the characters plus actors' names and the scenes they are in, notating all the costumes they wear for each act and scene, and where the quick changes occur.

Wings The area off stage right and left that is hidden from the audience, where the actors wait for their entrances and the props are set.

Wipe A drape that is usually walked across (but can be tracked) a scene or truck. *See also* Runner.

Working Drawings Drawings to scale of the set parts, that enable the workshop to build the set.

Working Lights Lights that are independent of the stage lights, usually switched on and off from the prompt corner. These are used when the stage lights are not needed, often during the day time when rehearsals or other work is happening on the stage.

INDEX